A taste of *Tidy Up or...*

"... About six months later I dropped Lyndsey a line on the dating site. I had a meeting near to where she lived and asked if she wanted to meet up for a reconciliatory drink. Her reply was that she would love to meet for a beer so she could throw it all over me. A firm refusal but, on reflection, fair."

Finding myself single at the age of forty was not in my life plan. I had never been very confident or particularly good at dating when I had youth and looks on my side. How the hell was I supposed to get back into meeting women now I was older, heavier, wrinklier and weighed down with emotional baggage?

This is the hilarious, odd, romantic and heartbreaking story of the crazy six years that followed. In search of the elusive next Mrs G I dated everyone from my closest friend's sister to a woman living in Moscow. I have online dated, speed dated and randomly chatted up hundreds of women, spent thousands of pounds and travelled thousands of miles.

After four years I began to think that there were no sane or balanced single women left on the planet. As years went by, however, the truth became inescapable. There was only one common factor linking all of these relationships and events together: ME! This painful lesson changed my life forever.

Join me as I reveal all ...

Logan,

Hope you enjoy it

Tidy Up on Your

Way Out

The hilarious true account of a

single man's search for love

Dave.

Dave Gammon

ISBN 978-1-491-05933-3

www.tidyuponyourwayout.com

ACKNOWLEDGEMENTS

This book would never have happened without:

A whole bunch of women who shared their hopes, dreams and desires in anything from a brief email to a year long relationship. I hope each and every one of you find what it is you seek and have beautiful lives.

Jennifer Manson (www.theflowwriter.com) - helping me get into the flow of the book and assisting me in navigating the process of book writing. You are a beautiful person.

Wanda Whiteley (www.manuscriptdoctor.co.uk) - for turning a jumble of words into something resembling a book and for your direct advice and counsel about the industry.

Lindsay Elliott – for contributing to the style and humour of the book and being a constant supporter and friend.

Dave Moore – for the website and book cover design. And for being the best friend a guy could have.

Samantha Lynch – for hours of patient transcription and having to cope with "weird" stuff about someone she knows well.

Angie Gammon – for feedback and encouragement from the other side of the world x.

The author would never have had the insight to tread his own path and write this book without:

Jamie Smart (www.jamiesmart.com) – my mentor and friend through a transitional time in my life.

Michael Neill (www.supercoach.com) – an inspiration for a better world.

Jim Rohn (www.jimrohn.com) – timeless wisdom from a man who I never met but whose words still leave a huge mark on my life.

Table of Contents

Prologue

Looking Back

The Rebound

Teenage Kicks

Electric Dreams

The Near Miss

With or Without You

Hot Fuzz

Pretty Polly

Mad Cow Disease

From Russia with Love

The Convenient Cat

Shitting on Your Own Doorstep

The Greek Travesty

Eyes Wide Shut

The Box of Frogs

Bridge over Troubled Waters

Swapping Teams

The Moratorium

Afterglow

"Your task is not to seek for love, but merely to seek and find all the barriers within yourself that you have built against it."

Rumi

"You know that look women give you when they want sex? ... Me neither."

Steve Martin

For Charlie and Tegwen – Missed in every moment.

Prologue

Being in a stranger's bathroom in the middle of the night is never a comfortable experience, but this one was just too quiet. I stared at my watch … 2.15am.

Nikki's toilet was located in a village somewhere north of Cardiff in the very quiet Welsh countryside. So far, our second date had gone well. She had got back from holiday that morning and was so keen to meet me that she had packed her daughter straight off to stay with Grandma. As for me, I had driven one hundred and eighteen miles to be with her, and although the journey had been hampered by a massive hangover, even my pounding head couldn't dampen my ardour as I ate up the miles on the M4.

I had wanted to be fresh-faced and full of the joys of spring for Nikki, but the previous evening, which had started out as a quiet drink catching up with my nephew, had ended up as a shot-fuelled frenzy wrapped off with a huge Doner Kebab and a short sleep on his settee.

Nikki and I had met online and had agreed to get together after having had a brief chat on the phone. Our first date was in Cardiff and we liked each other instantly. She was a bright, pretty, high-flying executive with a nice smile and a sexy Welsh accent. She had also been gifted with very significant breasts, so the cake had chocolate sprinkles from my perspective. She took me down to the Bay area for dinner and after that we got smashed on cocktails. Our drunken state inevitably ended up with our spending the night in what can best be described as "advanced cuddling".

After the first date, Nikki had mumbled about it all being "too much too soon", and this second date had pretty much followed the same trajectory. Once again, she resisted sex but cuddling her was nice, and as I'd jumped into bed beside her my eyes had caught sight of a few "interesting" bits of naughty reading on her bedside table. The stage was set for a great romance.

Three hours later, any thoughts of working through the Kama Sutra with her had left my mind. There were more pressing matters at hand. The sirloin steak washed down with Merlot, which I had been enjoying in the pub with Nikki, had joined forces with the various alcohols and kebab from the previous night. It was proving a very unholy alliance. Having not been gifted with the strongest of constitutions, this particular combination was taking my digestive system to the very edge of its performance envelope. Gravity had taken control and something was on the way out, and it was not possible to gauge with any confidence how noisy its final journey was going to be.

"Why is it so fucking quiet?" Sleep in my town-centre apartment is regularly disturbed by owls or low-flying helicopters from a nearby airbase, sounds I might normally associate with rural Wales. Right now, though, you could hear a flea fart.

I could wait no longer. With a bead of sweat dripping down my brow, like James Bond as he selected and cut the wire to switch off a ticking bomb, I relaxed the final muscles that were containing the potential holocaust. This was it.

I was out of luck. A massive report echoed round the bathroom (and I suspect the whole village), closely followed by a cacophony of gurgles and splashes as the previous twenty-four hours of excess tunefully liberated itself from my body.

"Fuck it! Fuck it!" I said to myself.

Perhaps Nikki never heard it. I calculated the distance to her head as probably around twelve feet and I was pretty sure she was facing the direction of the bathroom. I then dismally recalled that she had said "Are you OK?" and gently stroked my back as I'd got out of bed. The odds were not good.

Given the close proximity, I acted quickly with the air freshener to prevent a second sensual assault. Dismayed, I stayed slumped on the toilet trying to figure out my next move. As I did so, my mind drifted back to how I had ended up, forty-three years of age, skulking around a silent bathroom in a place I couldn't even name.

Looking Back

"I've been seeing somebody else." I scanned my wife Michelle's face but there were no indications that this was a joke.

I had known all day that a difficult discussion was coming, but I had not banked on the nuclear-scale impact of those five words.

That morning, feeling that something was brewing, I had been talking about the state of my marriage with Kate, my PA, but it had never occurred to me that Michelle would say this.

Kate had worked for me for the last five years and we had become close friends. She had a sharp mind and huge fawn-like eyes that I frequently found myself disappearing into whenever we did our morning diary check. She also had an annoyingly nice boyfriend she was engaged to.

She had asked me about my plans for the weekend. We were relaxing over a packet of cornflakes and a skimmed milk latte in the office canteen, something which had become a Friday morning tradition.

"I don't know, but I've a feeling Michelle and I are long overdue a serious conversation. I think our relationship could even end tonight."

Kate nearly jet-washed the wall, and me, with a stream of latte. This wasn't the normal banal list of chores (trip to Tesco, mow the lawn, drink wine, stroke cat) that made our conversations over breakfast so light-hearted. Shit was indeed happening and on a grand scale. She regained her composure, gently patted the milk from her chin, and asked what had happened.

In the spirit of dodging personal responsibility, I chose not to delve deeply into Michelle's and my eight years of monotonous marriage but instead chose the issue at the top of the list: a driving ban that had been gifted to me by the courts, as a result of my persistent speeding habit. Being the perceptive type, I had noticed a rapid deterioration in Michelle's mood over the period of the ban to the point where I would say our marriage had gone from its recent high point of "tedious" to a more serious status of "annoying/irritating".

I had been banned on 6th October for three months and Michelle had found nothing amusing in its fortuitous timing. Yes, it had been a crushing blow to my ego and my wallet, as well as presenting me with some huge logistical problems, but on the positive side I had been free to enjoy the Christmas festivities in an alcoholic haze. Who was going to drive to functions had been one of the regular flashpoints In our marriage and now there could be no argument. You would think this would have made for more cordial relations, but seemingly not.

Kate knew Michelle and was unsure of what to say, other than to tell me that it was all going to be alright and that it was most definitely a storm in a teacup. Just in case she was wrong, though, she also offered me the spare room in her house if I needed it. For the rest of the day I went about my working life putting the uneasy feeling that was growing inside me to the back of my mind.

Michelle and I had never been good at uncomfortable conversations. Our negotiating styles were too different. My preferred method is to attack and evade, bobbing and weaving my way towards scoring the point I am trying to win. In order to do this I need conversational space. Michelle was a master at blocking such space in an argument. There was right and there was wrong. The world of grey in which I tried to live did not exist for her. She would stand her ground, impervious to my punches, hitting me back with hard, fact-driven counter attacks. In most cases I simply ran out of energy and ended up losing the argument in the face of the simplest of facts from her, like pushing over an exhausted boxer with a single light shove. The concept of win-win outcomes did not exist in our communications.

As I pulled my car onto the drive (just two days after the return of my licence) I felt the butterflies in my stomach start to flutter wildly. Ahead of me, our large new-build Cotswold stone house stood imposing and uninviting. We'd bought it in a hurry when the lease on our flat had run out and it had always felt like a panic buy. For the last three years I had felt like I was living in someone else's house. The inside of the property had had little done to it, and had the feel of a show home.

As I walked through the front door and switched on the hall light, the magnolia walls and cream carpets almost blinded me. I made my way to the kitchen. As I passed the fridge I was tempted to spell out a message for Michelle from the hundreds of small white magnetic words on its chrome surface. That way, I could go to the pub, avoiding the uncomfortable discussion. Of course, I knew that wasn't really an option, and the words I would have needed weren't there in any case.

I opened the fridge door and pulled out a bottle of white wine. Michelle is very knowledgeable about wine. A visit to the Ideal Home Show earlier in the year meant that our garage was stocked with over two thousand pounds-worth. This particular bottle must have cost us thirty pounds, but I figured the situation warranted it. I relaxed at the sound of the wine splashing into the glass. If Michelle had been there she would have been telling me all about where it had come from and how long it had been stored, in what and by whom. She had an annoying habit of being able to retain all manner of information. This troubled me given the nature of the talk that was now long overdue between us.

I don't know what a thirty pound bottle of wine is supposed to taste like but it felt good as I swilled it round my mouth. I looked around the kitchen. We were not what you would call financially challenged. Michelle was a chartered accountant and a Cambridge graduate. I had left school at sixteen but had managed through most of our marriage to just about out-earn her, although it was always a close run thing.

Over the last twelve months we had spent a lot of money. This included a twenty thousand pound garden design, five holidays and a whole bunch of other stuff. Michelle had bought a four hundred pound cardigan in a retail therapy moment that shocked even me. Our marriage would never end because of financial pressure, but the spending was a symptom of something that wasn't working in it. I don't know at what precise point unhappiness set in for me. It may even have been before we were married.

I heard Michelle's key in the lock and her footsteps in the hall. My butterflies returned and I stood up, unsure of what to do. I knew the situation required a strong opening but I couldn't seem to frame the words. Michelle came into the kitchen and just as I was ready to speak she shot me a glance and said "We need to talk."

This was not in the script and for a moment I didn't know where to go next. I fetched her a wine glass.

"Yes, you're right. It'll be good to talk things through."

Before I had even picked up the wine bottle to pour six pounds' worth of alcohol into her glass she dropped her bombshell.

"I've been seeing somebody else."

It was the pre-emptive punch that instantly stole my moment. The bitch, I thought to myself.

What happened next surprised me so I am sure it must have shocked her. A giggle escaped my lips.

"So there was me thinking you were just being shitty because I'd been banned from driving. When all the time you've been with someone else."

Then the obvious question that would occur to any male: "Do I know him?"

I did. It was Chris from her office. We had met once when he came to the house and although I remember being irritated at how he always directed his answers to Michelle whenever I asked him a question, he hadn't seemed a threat. He had struck me as something of a knob-head. He was an actuary, which is not a profession renowned for being populated with exciting people. He was also a passionate fly fisherman, seemingly with no desire to spend his spare time on anything else.

This had clearly been a stealth attack. Chris had sneaked in under my radar and stolen my wife. Not particularly good news for my ego but I figured I would have to deal with that another day.

I resorted to brute force. "Well, you might as well fuck off then."

Michelle didn't look surprised. We had discussed fidelity in the context of friends and family so many times that she knew that telling me she had been unfaithful would be terminal. She walked out of the kitchen and went upstairs to get a few things from the bedroom. I could hear her opening and closing drawers and then the sound of her footsteps on the stairs as she struggled with her bag. Meanwhile, I stood staring out of the kitchen window into the darkness trying to work out how in the space of a few minutes my whole life had fallen apart.

After the front door slammed, I stood for some while staring at the reflection of the man in the window. A year shy of forty, fat, wearing boring middle-aged clothes, with a tear-stained face. I pulled away only when I realised that my wine glass was empty.

Later, there were a few frantic calls to my closest friends and more wine. (The most expensive stuff was going down well as break-up wine.) Eventually, some way through the second bottle, everything became a blur.

As I slept I felt her move close. She cuddled up and I nestled into her comforting warmth and felt the wetness of her lips as they passed over my cheeks. The sensation slowly pulled me into consciousness and blearily I peered into a dark strange world. I was not in my bed; I didn't know where I was. I felt her warm softness against me and as our eyes met I smiled. She purred. Sometime in the night my cat had come to check on my wellbeing, curious to discover why the sleeping arrangements had changed.

My brain slowly started to re-assemble what was in front of my eyes. I realised that my face was lying on a cream carpet and as the image came into focus I recognized, albeit at an odd angle, the cold marble of the living room fireplace. With a supreme effort I raised my head to look at the clock. It was 2am so I must have slept for a good few hours. There was some good news. Half of my body had managed to stay on the sofa, but the downside was that the combination of two expensive bottles of wine and the vast bulk of my blood being in my head meant that as consciousness increased so did the realization that I was in pain. As I pulled myself up, the full extent of the hangover hit me like a lorry. I got to my feet and strolled to the kitchen, clutching the wall for support as I went. I poured a glass of water and gulped it down to relieve the burning dryness of my throat. After refilling my glass I climbed the stairs to bed.

I went into the bedroom but all of her things were still there so I made my way to the guest room. The moment I lay down on the bed my mind kicked in and began to replay the events of the previous evening. I searched for answers to a question I should have been asking myself years ago. I kept thinking of the two of them cuddling in his bed, laughing about the evening's events and it tortured me until the alcohol finally slipped me into sleep. This was it. I was single again.

TIDY UP ON YOUR WAY OUT

The Rebound

Over the weeks following my marriage breakdown I made some desperate attempts at reconciliation, including begging Michelle to give it another chance. She didn't take the bait and deep inside I was glad. Even if I was miserable at that moment, it was obvious to me that the right thing had happened. Perhaps I knew the clouds would soon pass.

I had an interesting conversation with my boss. He wasn't generally a people kind of person so I found this a little odd until he opened up that there had been some challenges in his marriage too. This was to become a trend among people I spoke to. Once you find yourself in the "recently separated" category, they tend to feel obliged to offload their marital problems onto you. After a while it began to piss me off. It felt like they were stealing my grief. It was interesting though. I'd never realised how many marriages seemed to be happily gliding along on the surface looking beautiful, while below the waterline they were fraught with problems.

It was worth putting up with my boss's interrogation because at the end of it he told me to take a week off.

I spent the week going to the gym and putting my affairs in order. On Wednesday morning the cleaner turned up. The word "cleaner" usually conjures up an image of a Hilda Ogden-type character, but ours was young and fit. She gave a start when she saw me.

"Hi, I didn't expect to see you here."

I told her that Michelle had left me and that I'd been given a week off work and she made tea while I told her the whole story. We talked for hours (she still did the cleaning in case you were worried), and it felt good to offload about the break up on an impartial party, especially when she revealed that she had always liked me more than Michelle anyway.

As she left, she said, "I'm thinking of going down the pub tomorrow night. Do you want to come?"

I jumped at the chance. Sitting at home was doing me no good. I have a tendency of getting caught up in my own thinking and beating myself up, so any distraction at that point would have been warmly welcomed, and a fit female one especially so.

We got quite drunk at the pub the next evening. She came back to mine for coffee and we ended up spending the night together although we were both too pissed for things to get too out of hand. I had conflicted feelings: on the one hand there was guilt that I was doing this such a short time since separating (even though Michelle had been at it for months); on the other, I was thinking, "This is the coolest thing ever". Only four days in, and I had the confidence boost I needed.

It allowed me to hope that women might still find me attractive. It also provided my friends with a cue for a stream of cleaning-related jokes, a personal favourite being "Did she polish your Mr Muscle?"

After a week of being single I had a call out of the blue from my friend Alex.

"Mate, I'm back in the country. What's been happening?"

Alex and I had met when we were partnered together on a rock climbing course ten years ago. There is a unique bond of friendship between us, strengthened by literally hanging onto each other's lives while climbing. The last time I had seen him was two years before. There was a great deal of good fortune in his timing. I was lonely, he was free to come and stay, and no sooner had I explained recent events to him than he was on a train heading to my place.

One evening, as we were walking back from a boozy pub dinner, Alex said something that changed my whole thinking about the separation:

"Dave, do you realise what this split-up means? You now get to do what you want, when you want."

Until now, my desperation to get back into a marriage I was not enjoying was driven by two things: wounded pride and being out of my comfort zone. Suddenly possibilities opened up before me. Go on holiday where I want, be with whom I want, live where I want. Shit, I could even leave the toilet seat up.

It was not even two weeks since I had split up with Michelle and as I looked at the rolling hills stretching down to the Severn Estuary, I realised that not only was I going to be alright, but that this was going to be amazing.

The following weekend Alex and I drove down to Essex. My best friend Paul had organised a separation party, the final goodbye to my old life, and all my friends were going to come out and play. This prestigious event was to take place at a wanky old working mans club because the evening was coinciding with one of his band's gigs. The location did not matter. What did was that a whole bunch of my friends turned up and we all hit it hard. So hard in fact that I had lost the power of coherent speech by about 9pm, let alone any sense of where I was.

I was on such a high that I tried chatting up a really gorgeous-looking girl who I'd seen at gigs before. I didn't care that she was completely thick. Mental stimulation wasn't a short-term priority. I figured I could always pay to hire a female university graduate to talk to me about current affairs and scientific breakthroughs, like an intellectual prostitute.

My efforts were unsuccessful, due in no short measure to her husband being at the gig. But it still felt good to get some practice in.

After the gig one of my friends managed to blag us a table for ten at a Chinese restaurant that was about to close its doors for the night. As I sat there, totally hammered, I looked around me. I was surrounded by the best people in my world, eating some great food, and in that moment I was the happiest man alive. All of the worries and stresses of the previous weeks had fallen away.

The next evening I went to another of Paul's gigs. This time it was in Basildon, the spiritual homeland of the Essex girl. Having spent a large part of my life around Essex girls I have always felt an affinity with them. All I see is women who happen to care about their appearance. Whilst there are some who are intellectually challenged I have never found this to be in any way disproportionate to other parts of the country.

I was at the bar talking with a friend for reasons that even today I still find baffling, about the relative merits of different pension plans, when my eye was caught by a group of girls. I don't know how our conversation had led to pensions, but it was not good for a Saturday night, so I found myself increasingly distracted by them. One of the girls was sneaking furtive glances in my direction. At first I assumed she was looking at someone else and I turned around to check out who was behind me. I didn't want to grin like a moron at her only to be labelled weird.

There was no one there; she was looking at me. The next time she looked at me I rolled my eyes in an expression intended to let her know I was fuckin' bored with my current conversation. She smiled. Oh my good god. I excused myself to my friend and approached her, bold as day. Luckily she turned towards me so I didn't have to use my contingency plan which would have had me walking past her and into the toilets.

"Hi, can I buy you a drink so I can have someone else to talk to? My friend is boring me rigid."

That is how I met Rachel.

Rachel had big brown eyes and a smile that made me want to hold her forever. A Basildon girl, born and bred, with three children, she worked in a local school as a Teaching Assistant. We didn't talk for long that evening, but we spoke on the phone the next day and arranged to meet up.

It was the first time I had dated someone who had children so I was not used to the whole fortnightly custody cycle. Rachel's ex-husband had them every other weekend (and for some reason believed this put him in line for some sort of father of the year award) and it was on these weekends that Rachel was free to go out and play.

Our first date never actually happened. Half way round the M25 Rachel phoned to say her daughter had broken a tooth and they had to go to the emergency dentist. She sounded as disappointed as I was which helped me bear the whole thing with dignity.

I realised that it was the first time that someone's children had got in the way of my plans. It's hard to believe, but although I was in my late thirties I had managed to avoid the hassle and turmoil that seem to accompany the introduction of children into my life. I had managed thus far to evade the world of cosy families, the wiping of kids' noses and other orifices. I was responsible for one person: me, and I spent my spare time and income on things I wanted.

In many ways, I had always looked on somewhat bemused at my friends as they ran round after their kids, chauffeuring them and clearing up after them. It had always seemed to me like they were surrendering their own quality of life in favour of their children's'. Whilst I had Sunday lunch in quiet, elegant hotel restaurants they would be chasing their children out of the soft play area of a Harvester, having to grab mouthfuls of below-average roast chicken whilst force-feeding chicken nuggets into the unwilling traps of their minors. In short, children had never been high on my agenda.

Two weeks after the aborted date I set off again to Basildon. As part of my separation recovery plan I had got a new car from the company car pool, a gleaming silver Mercedes. It looked good and I felt good as I headed out to Essex. It was now over a month since our one and only meeting. I was a little anxious. Was Rachel really as good looking as I remembered or had beer goggles played a part in my recollection of her?

Any doubts I had disappeared as she came out of her house and opened the passenger door. We set out to a country pub I knew well, and although it was only a short drive that I had done countless times I was so distracted talking to Rachel that I got hopelessly lost on the way.

An hour later than planned, we were finally able to continue our conversation in the pub over a couple of glasses of wine. We sat close to each other by the fire and as she spoke about her three children and her husband's affairs (after the second she gave him his marching orders, happily for me) I couldn't help staring at her like a pet stares at its owner while they are eating dinner.

The evening went by in a flash and before I knew it I was pulling up outside Rachel's house. She invited me in for coffee and we sat and chatted for a while. Then it happened. We kissed. Oh my god. I had forgotten the sheer delight a good snog brings. Michelle had not been mad on kissing and this was the first lingering, full-on kiss I had enjoyed for the best part of nine years. Kissing creates a feeling of connection that cannot be beaten by anything.

We snogged like rampant teenagers until well past 3am. When I left to drive home I was completely giddy. It was obvious to me that I had fallen head over heels in love with her.

The two weeks before we got to meet again were the slowest of my life. We had arranged that Rachel would spend the weekend at my house in Gloucestershire. As she didn't drive, I got up early and drove one hundred and sixty miles to Essex, picked her up and drove straight back again. It was economic and environmental madness but I didn't give a shit. I was just happy to be with her.

Back home, we drank a few bottles of Michelle's Ideal Home Show wine, talked and played music. We had planned to eat at the local pub but we were so chilled out we ordered pizzas and stayed in. We made love most of the night in a rare display of longevity on my part. A long lazy Sunday morning followed. Everything about the weekend was perfect.

The fortnightly pattern of seeing each other continued for a few months until Rachel felt it was a good time to meet the kids. I knew it was a huge deal for her. I didn't know what to expect so didn't worry about it.

The children were waiting at Rachel's mum's house, perched in a neat line on the sofa, along with Rachel's sisters and all of their children. I finally knew what it felt like to be an auction lot paraded in front of everyone. I was happy, though, as I knew that this meant I could now see Rachel on weekends she had the children. What I didn't know was that this presented a new and unforeseen hurdle.

Up until this point I can safely say I have never had, or contemplated, sex within earshot of minors. The proximity of the children's bedrooms to Rachel's had me almost paralysed the first night I stayed over. Not quite to the point of not being able to have sex (only the children dancing on the bed would have had the power to stop me) but it was awkward. Rachel did not seem at all concerned, probably because she was familiar with her children's nocturnal patterns and knew the point when nothing would wake them.

I never did get used to it. These nights became a tortuous tightrope walk between my carnal urges and the fear of being overheard. Or even worse, the dreaded "walk-in". Sometimes a small noise, a child's moan or cough, had me leaping off and pretending to be asleep in mid-sexual flight.

Days with Rachel's children began to reveal some things about me that created the finest hairline cracks in our otherwise flawless relationship. The older two were absolutely fine around me but her youngest daughter was clearly struggling with the whole idea.

Gradually, I found myself getting into an escalating power struggle for Rachel's attention with her daughter. My attempts at trying to build a friendship with her were repeatedly thwarted. She would ruthlessly compete for the settee space next to her mother, and as she cuddled Rachel, she would often steal me furtive "fuck you" glances to demonstrate that she knew exactly what she was doing. I tried the cinema, meals out, bowling and walks in the park to win her over, but all to no avail.

I decided I was going to pull out all the stops and planned a trip to Chessington World of Adventures during the children's summer holidays. Chessington happens to be the ultimate manifestation of my own personal vision of hell on earth. A sea of kids, high on sugar and crap fatty fast foods, sprinting around screaming, crying, puking and kicking off whilst I would have to queue endlessly for some two-minute thrill ride. But as this was my final chance for a relationship with the children, hey.

As I sat in traffic in a borrowed "family-friendly car" (How do family cars manage to get as deeply filthy as they do? I exchanged my gleaming and spotless new Audi convertible with one of my colleagues' family saloons and I felt like I was driving around in a wheeled skip.) the children were already showing signs of early boredom setting in. Then, once we were at Chessington, Rachel's youngest daughter seemed to have come up with a devious plan of action, designed to guarantee my reconciliation day would be ruined. We queued for thirty minutes at a huge slide, only for her to lose her bottle at the last second and return to her mother in floods of tears. The warm weather and sickly presence of sugar everywhere had brought a miniature plague of wasps to the park. This could not have worked out better for her. She screamed at the mere notion of their presence, which grew in volume if a wasp dared to get remotely close to her. There was a point where I had to put myself in a meditative state to prevent myself pushing her face into her pizza. I knew she was trying to draw a reaction from me and I was only a hair's breadth away from demonstrating my own preferred parental style. It took all my strength, but I managed to hold off, as I knew that it would make the whole day an unmitigated failure, and I didn't want to give her the satisfaction of that victory.

By the time we got back to the house in Essex I was a physical and emotional wreck. Rachel tried to console me by telling me that the children had loved the whole day but I was beyond caring. She saw in my eyes that I had given up any hope of spending quality time around her children.

Any problems I was having trying to be the family man were further exacerbated by Rachel's dickhead of an ex. Although he was responsible for the infidelity that resulted in the end of their marriage he was convinced somehow that he was the wronged party. Jason tried everything to make our lives absolute hell. I understood his jealousy, having lost Michelle to another man, but Jason did nothing to control his primeval response to finding out that someone whom he had had sex with actually had the nerve to sleep with someone else. Any sympathy I had for him dried up the moment his dummy spitting actions began to impinge on my relationship with Rachel.

It was not long before things started to get stupid. Soon Rachel found herself having to lie to the children about what we were doing because if word got back to Jason that I was planning something nice he would scupper it by cancelling having the children at the last minute. He texted Rachel continuously, demanding to know what was going on between us and asking her to give things another go. She tried to hide what was going on to spare me the worst of it but I could see it was wearing her down.

I finally lost it the day I bought her son tickets to see Arsenal play a game at the Emirates Stadium. My nephew had tracked them down and Rachel's boy was thrilled to bits. Jason went mad. Apparently it was a rite of passage for every dad to take his son to his first football game. To be fair I agreed with that, mainly because I hate football, but I found myself biting back the retort that it was obviously not an important rite if Jason hadn't bothered with it in the first thirteen years of his son's life.

I had to sit there while Jason shouted at Rachel down the phone. She would not pass it to me so that I could speak to him so I had to communicate via her. I told Rachel to ask him if he wanted the tickets, which would save me the trouble of going, but apparently he was not prepared to accept "charity from him". (I suspect there were a couple of nouns used instead of the word "him" but Rachel was applying a filter to the translation). After that I offered an alternative olive branch: that I should tear up the tickets up in front of his son and explain that his father would not let me take him. This option was not relayed to Jason.

Back in Gloucestershire there was a lot going on in my life. I had been approached by another company to work for them in Windsor and as the marital home had finally sold I was able to buy a flashy new apartment in Hampshire with my share of the proceeds. It was closer to Rachel, and she could catch a train to Windsor which made things a whole lot easier. Everything appeared to be going to plan.

We continued to see each other whenever we could, and when it was just the two of us there wasn't a ruffle to spoil our happiness. One Friday evening in October, as we were walking home from the pub, I broached the subject of Christmas. It was to be the first that her ex was going to have the children and Rachel was at a loss as to what to do. I could see that the idea of not being with them was upsetting her.

I came up with a plan. She would spend Christmas Eve and Christmas Day at my apartment and then I would then drive her back to Essex on Boxing Day to be with her family. Even Jason couldn't fuck this one up. To backtrack on a commitment to having the children at Christmas was too monstrous an act even by his standards. I figured, because of this, that I would be safe to pull out all the stops and give Rachel the best Christmas I possibly could.

So it came to pass that I collected Rachel from Slough station on the afternoon of Christmas Eve. My apartment was beautifully decorated and I had been out and completed my first ever solo Christmas food shopping sortie. Fresh turkey crown from the butcher's, the lot.

On Christmas day I woke up before Rachel and lay there looking at her while she slept. I thought of everything she did, and everything she was: how she managed to hold down a job, keep a house and raise three children with limited support, all the while keeping happy-go-lucky, positive and beautiful. My heart was full.

That day we opened presents, ate lunch, listened to music, drank champagne and made love until time ran out on us.

Driving back to Essex on Boxing Day, I could feel some of the veneer rubbing off and it made me feel troubled. As I saw it, the life I really wanted was being snatched away and put in a box for another day when I might be allowed to glimpse it briefly. Would there come a point when I had to make choice between the person I loved and the life I wanted?

When I got back to my apartment I felt very lonely.

My days with Rachel never again scaled the heady heights of that stolen Christmas. A few months later, as summer got closer, my thoughts turned to a holiday. I longed to take Rachel away. I was not enjoying my new job, and felt stressed and angry much of the time. It was, however, paying well so I asked Rachel to choose somewhere she had always wanted to go and I would take her there.

Rachel procrastinated like a professional. She would not be drawn into a commitment. Even at the point where the "when" was agreed, I still couldn't get a decision from her on the "where". As the days counted down Rachel continued to avoid the issue. Even though she knew I would be paying for it, she couldn't help feeling guilty about going on an expensive holiday without her children.

In the end, we ran out of time and ended up having a few days in a hotel in Bath. After our mini-break things never felt the same for me. I brooded at home while Rachel took the children away to Spain for a week with her sister, asking myself if I was mature or unselfish enough to make the relationship work. I knew that this was how life was going to be if we stayed together and my mind churned over the evidence that it wouldn't work: the physical distance, her not being able to drive, a nagging belief that it was a "rebound" relationship, the children, and our different worlds. Rachel picked up on my mood and our phone conversations grew strained while she was away and by the time she was due home I had made my mind up to end the relationship, no matter how heart-breaking it would be. As it turned out, it was a lot more painful than my separation from Michelle had been.

One thing I had learned from Michelle was that a decapitation strategy was better that death by a thousand cuts so I broke up with Rachel by phone. I knew that if I tried to do it face to face it would not work. Paul, who saw Rachel every now and then at his gigs, was highly critical of my decision to end the relationship that way, but I really didn't see any alternative at the time.

This is a particular form of guilt I was soon going to learn to live with.

TIDY UP ON YOUR WAY OUT

Teenage Kicks

My dating prowess as a fourteen year old was legendary. Legendary for being shit. I could not have been less confident with girls if I'd tried. Judging by the amount of time I spent hanging around with them at school and the growing tissue pile under the bed it was evident that I was definitely interested in girls, but whatever I had learned about sex and women as a child had done nothing to propel me into the Premier Division of popular boys at school.

Mostly, I managed to achieve an air of boisterous self-confidence around the fairer sex but it was actually a cunning disguise. Underneath was a crippling fear of rejection which led me to avoid the discussion or practice of sex.

My senior school frustration was at its peak when a girl called Louise started to show an interest in me. We sat opposite each other twice a week in Biology (the irony of it kills me to this day), separated by a porcelain sink and, on occasion, a Bunsen burner. She was petite and very funny with dark curly hair and dancing eyes. A deadly combination of attraction and fear drove me crazy for a full year and the fact that she was not backwards about coming forward only added to my terror.

My interest in Louise was further complicated by her dating my friend for a while. Having to listen to his graphic accounts of early fumblings and sexual encounters with the girl of my dreams heaped fuel on the flames. I was mesmerised by her.

You would have thought that the endless attention Louise gave me and the regular questioning from her friends about whether I fancied her would have given me sufficient bottle to ask her out, but I've never been very good at reading signals of interest from girls.

In retrospect, I think Louise destroyed my life in many ways, not least the result of my failing to achieve even a mediocre CSE result in Biology, thus ending any aspiration I had for a career in veterinary practice which I have long suspected would have been the perfect job for me.

About four years into my marriage there was a social revolution as the Friends Reunited website was launched onto an unsuspecting world. It was the first of the social media sites that enabled people to connect with everyone from their past, including old school flames. It is well documented that the launch of the site coincided with a big spike in the UK divorce rate as waves of bored and disillusioned marrieds relit the romantic embers of their playground days.

The day I accepted a 'friend request' from Louise sowed the seed for some future entanglement. I was in my unhappily married phase at the time and although our messages would occasionally get a bit saucy, I kind of knew where the line was (and only hopped over it every now and again). Frankly, the attention was a welcome distraction.

As for Louise, she was single but had been seeing a guy who was clearly using her for sex. I fell into the familiar role of 'agony uncle' and listened to her pouring her heart out, empathising and sympathising in equal measure, whilst thinking how much I would like to be in her boyfriend's shoes for a while. I am a good agony uncle, due in part to my early fear of asking girls for a date. I was used to playing the long game: becoming friends and then trying to work towards underwear privileges from that position. It was an endless, hard road that frequently ended in disappointment. It may have been admirable in intent but it was largely useless as a strategy. It also meant that I ended up dealing with all the shit parts of a woman's relationship while some other bloke happily got his rocks off, thanks in no small part to my counselling and coaching of his girlfriend.

Louise and I did contemplate meeting up. At one point there was even a plan to meet for dinner at the Edgware Road Hilton where I was staying for work. In the end, though, I got cold feet and Louise decided that her prick of a boyfriend was more sincere than she'd thought (it was to be a few years before my opinion was finally vindicated but I still take some satisfaction in my diagnosis being spot on) so my fantasy of dinner followed by the subtle suggestion that we should retire to my room, pausing for a passionate kiss in the elevator en-route, was destined to remain just that.

When my split with Michelle happened, Louise stepped into the agony aunt role for me. She did it really well, in spite of her own problems, but still we never met. (By now she was dating another loser called Craig who was probably a whole book in his own right.) Now I was single, fantasies of my childhood sweetheart were becoming more regular in my head, but then I met Rachel so Louise and I switched back to being counsellors whenever the need arose.

In a fortunate twist of fate a short window opened where Louise and I were both single.

An argument with Rachel had left me bereft for a short while and Louise's emotional scars from her split with Craig were finally healing over. We decided we both needed cheering up and arranged to meet for Saturday night dinner and booze.

As I sprinted around the M25 it occurred to me that I hadn't actually seen Louise for at least 20 years. In my head she was still the fifteen-year-old schoolgirl, her crystal-blue eyes gently sparkling in the light of the Bunsen burner. I wondered if meeting her would be a colossal mistake and if my schoolboy fantasy bubble was about to be pricked by the needle of reality, but when I weighed it up I figured that if it was the case, at least I would be able to move on and forget my silly childhood crush once and for all.

The day hadn't had an auspicious start. That morning I had received a text from Louise saying she had just had to have her dog put down. Such an event has been known to kill passion stone dead. When my cat was in for a routine overnight operation I couldn't even look at my girlfriend, let alone stir the trouser beast into action. Did it work like this for women as well? I wasn't necessarily expecting a sexual outcome to the evening but should the necessary chemical attraction happen I didn't want other distractions getting in the way. I offered to defer to another evening but Louise was adamant that it would do her good to meet up.

As I walked up the path to her door I steeled myself. Technically this was a blind date and I was fully prepared to adopt my much-practiced "delighted" facial expression that I can turn on in the most horrific of encounters when required. The frosted glass in her front door delayed the unveiling a few seconds longer but then the door opened and there she stood.

She had barely changed. Her face was immediately recognisable with only a few wrinkles around the eyes giving away the years that had passed since our last meeting. Her breasts were definitely bigger than I remembered but I couldn't really calculate with any precision whether this was a spatial illusion or, as I was later to jokingly accuse her of, a work of surgical wonder. She wasn't in her school uniform but I guess that would have been a big ask for a first date.

We sat in Louise's living room with a glass of wine and both of us were a little lost for words. We spent half an hour repeating variations on the sentence "You don't look any different," whilst staring intently at each other, trying to find more changes. I have plenty of pictures of me as a kid and I know damn well I don't look anything like that, but for her it was clearly a step back in time.

Over dinner, I detected a glimmer of sadness in Louise's eyes which I put down to the whole dog thing. There was only one thing for it; I ordered a round of champagne cocktails. My relationship with champagne is, to be fair, a mixed bag. I love the stuff but it has a range of effects on me from "happy drunk" through "charming raconteur" to "sexually impotent". It was my Russian roulette dating drink but if it made Louise smile it was a risk worth taking.

Many champagne cocktails later we were both absolutely hammered, stuffed full of tapas and getting bored with saying how neither of us had changed. In between all of this, I had learned a fair bit about some of my old school friends and teachers but the champagne ensured none of the information remained in my head the next morning.

On the way home, we had one cheeky snog in the cab. Once through the door, I stumbled into the kitchen to pour some more wine. Louise disappeared upstairs, appearing a few minutes later naked under a dressing gown. She gave me a look that was pure 4th Grade biology flirt and whether it was the champagne, the pet-related grief, or just a journey back in time it all kicked off in a frenzy. We made out on the settee, on the floor, on the kitchen surface (first time on a semi-hygienic surface so a big tick in the box there) before finally getting into bed and carrying on my schoolboy fantasy.

It was a drunken outpouring of over twenty years of pent-up sexual desire. My only wish was that there had been a test-tube or dissected frog for added effect. As we kissed and generally engaged in the practice of those biological principles we had learned together two decades before, I remember thinking that in my head I had a completely different idea of what this was going to be like. Not better, just different, and it bothered me.

The next morning my head hurt ... BAD, and judging by her face, Louise was in a similar place. For a moment I thought I detected a look of embarrassment, possibly even disapproval, on her face but I think I was mistaken. We sat in bed for hours, talking and drinking tea. I caught up on what had happened to so and so from school that had not locked in the previous night, then the combination of my irrational habit of wanting sex when hung-over and Louise's nakedness proved irresistible and we made love. It validated for me that the events of the previous night hadn't just been about alcohol and mourning, that there was a genuine chemistry between us.

And yet I felt it was all wrong. You see, Louise, unlike me, hadn't left home. She had firmly stayed in our Essex hometown, buying a house half a mile from the one in which she was born and even working at the school we both went to. She was a beautiful connection to the past and yet I wasn't sure I was ready to be reconnected with my history.

Something could have developed from that night and yet it never did. I was still smarting over my argument with Rachel and I think Louise was confused about Craig. Months later, Louise visited me in Hampshire and we had a lovely evening with yet more champagne. She slept in my bed with me but we never had sex. I would love to say how beautiful it was that she trusted me and felt able to cuddle me all night. For me, however, the experience was a sleepless night with a duvet tent going on.

Louise eventually met and married a guy many years her junior and had a child with him. She seems happy and content and all is good in her life. We still keep in contact but we politely avoid the subject of our evening together. She had told me that she had wanted to go out with me at school and I had a 'Sliding Doors' moment of wondering what would have happened if we had. Maybe our evening together had been our consolation prize.

TIDY UP ON YOUR WAY OUT

Electric Dreams

I was grateful for the social lifeline Paul's gigs offered me. Without it I would be doing the same as all my other male friends: staying at home being a husband and a father. (The only difference was that I didn't have children or a wife.) However, after a few months, I realised that this particular gene pool was too small. More often than not, I was finding myself in the company of the same women, and the attractive ones were either in a relationship or had made it abundantly clear that they were not interested in me. With the shortage of dateable women, the distance I had to travel, and the wounds I still felt after Rachel, I was reluctant to date "Essex" for a while.

The workplace should, by rights, be a rich hunting ground for me. In my twenties, I had met both Michelle and Sally, a previous long-term girlfriend, at work but now I was on a higher rung of the corporate ladder. Given my position, I felt it would be inappropriate to engage in emotional entanglements. I don't know if there was any sense in this, but it was a policy I maintained, probably to my sexual cost.

Now I was close to forty the tactics employed by my youthful Essex boy incarnation were likely to be of limited value. Things had changed. I was not about to try pulling a toothbrush out of my pocket and telling a girl 'Get your coat, you've pulled.' Nor would I engage in a 'pull a pig' night as a means of building confidence. Neither seemed appropriate or funny any more.

I read a few books about dating and pick-up techniques and while some of the ideas proved useful, something felt unnatural and contrived about the whole systemised approach to initiating contact, building rapport, and closing to a next step. It all sounded like a sales training course. My success with Rachel had made me confident that if I could only get in front of the right woman I would be okay. I have always been nervous of making the approach or asking for a number, but I knew that no amount of books on tactics would ever make me any better at it. I just had to bite the bullet and push through my fears.

The last time I had been involved in dating, the idea of a dating agency had been taboo and certainly not something you would tell people about. The emergence of online dating sites had changed all of that, and even men seemed quite happy to openly share their experiences of searching for women. It had to be worth a try.

One rainy Saturday afternoon I finally sat down with my laptop and began to go through the wealth of online dating sites available. It just seemed too easy. A simple registration and then thousands of hot single women immediately within your field of vision, appearing out of every nook and cranny. There was even a stack of single women within a five mile radius of my apartment, and most of them looked drop-dead gorgeous. I didn't subscribe for a few days, instead taking advantage of the trial periods to explore the women's profiles. I was like some sort of weird online peeping tom and it was strangely addictive; like going through the Great Universal catalogue as a child, in order to write your Christmas list.

The following weekend I finally committed to two dating sites and spent the afternoon getting my profile in shape. I selected the best recent pictures that I could find and crafted a profile that gave a balanced and honest view of me. I pressed submit and sat back. Now the trap was set, all I had to do was wait for the winks and messages to come flooding in.

A few days went by and having not had a single indication of interest, I went in to check that my account was actually active. A few people had looked at my profile, but other than that nothing. I then spent an evening going through a search of women within a ten mile radius and embarked on a massive wave of winking and messaging, the latter personalised for maximum effectiveness. Days passed and still nothing. Something was wrong.

I decided to do something more proactive, and my alter ego "Davina Brahms" set her profile up on Dating Direct a few days later. She was thirty eight, from Basingstoke, and a figment of my imagination. She was looking for a fun-loving guy aged between forty and forty-three. Davina was my way of checking out the competition (sorry Ray from Crowthorne but I hope you understand why there was no reply now). She helped me uncover the missing link.

I discovered that compared with all the other guys' profiles mine was far too truthful. I quickly set about immediate damage rectification, changing my profile to one that was a loveable, kind to animals and old people, rugged, adventurous, superhero-like, romantic, puppy-saved-from-burning-building kind of guy. In short, the man from the razor advert (like every other lying fucker on the site). I chose new pictures that regressed a few years but reflected how I would look again one day, once my gym and diet regime finally kicked in.

I was inundated with replies within a few hours, or at least as inundated as men get on dating sites. Women are generally bombarded with messages and winks, which is something that has never happened to me or most of the men I know who date online.

I like to think that it is because chivalry is not dead in the online world and that men are still expected to make the first move, and not because I am not as much of a catch as I like to think.

The online dating world is caught up in its own colossal catch 22 situation. If you don't lie about your build and personality, and upload old pictures showing yourself when you were slim and attractive, you will not get any responses. Our expectations are so ridiculously high that we need to lie just to get to first base.

Now, at last, my outbound messages were getting a response in about one in three instances. My conversion rate from email response to date was pretty much 100%. As long as I managed to hook someone into a conversation, I would be sure of a dating opportunity. But it wasn't long before I took a few big hits to my confidence.

Karen broke my internet cherry. We got into an intense conversation very quickly and emailed each other for hours. Within the space of two days I had got to know a lot about her and it naively felt like we had an instant, deep connection. We exchanged a few more photographs and spoke on the phone. In short, we got on well. I was swept away with the excitement of it all. Then, just as we were about to arrange our first date, she sent me an email saying that her ex had been in touch and wanted to talk about a reconciliation.

I was surprisingly upset at having been dumped by someone I had never met. For days I had that empty feeling in my stomach that comes when something I really want is snatched away. It took me many years and a lot of heartache to learn how unwise it is to get attached to the idea of a person, rather than the actual thing.

My next internet disaster was Sophie. Having been all keen and eager in her emails and on the phone, she took offence at a picture I sent. To be accused of not being as attractive as I had supposedly made myself out to be was not the sort of knock someone early in their online dating career could easily brush off. The action of writing someone off, based on a single photograph, shows the worrying degree of shallowness that online dating has created in people, including myself .

Some years later I was to nod enthusiastically when my friend Billy told me of his golden rule: "If they don't have more than one picture, don't respond." There is an elegant logic behind this principle. If you can't find a few decent pictures of yourself to put on a dating site then you are either not as attractive as you would like people to believe or are not getting out often enough to get in pictures. As a further extension to this rule I also ignore professionally taken photographs. The rise in popularity of makeover photography sessions, however innocent the motive, has resulted in a surge in dating site fraud. A photographer can make any old boiler look good with a splurge of makeup and clever lighting.

These early rejections confirmed what has remained true to this day: I am uncomfortable with the very idea of online dating. To me it defies the natural order of things;: that order being:

1. Meet someone
2. Find them attractive
3. Get to know them
4. Like them
5. Fall in Love

Any alternative approach or change in the above order does not tend to work well for me. This is because I am a "switch" kind of guy. There are two types of people who inhabit this planet: "switches" and "dials". The cool thing about being a dial is that there are several settings. For example, you can like someone just a little bit and then gradually turn up the dial. Or it can go the other way: you can lose a bit of feeling for someone but still have enough in the tank to keep the relationship moving forward.

I am a switch. There are two settings to a switch: "on" and "off". If I like someone, it is an immediate and intense sensation. As a result, my online dating tends to go like this:

1. Meet someone

all in Love

_. Get to know them

4. Fall out of love / get dumped

I like being a switch person because I enjoy the rollercoaster of emotion that comes with it. The sensational highs and crushing lows are all part of life for me. Because of this, I have to be very choosy about whom I engage in conversation online because once the switch flicks I am "all in", and at serious risk of getting an emotional kick in the pods.

I made a real point of paying attention to what women said about themselves in their profiles. Before I was to commit I needed to know my facts and be certain we would make a good combination. Predictably, I soon discovered that women were as full of shit as men when it came to describing themselves. Particularly irritating were the "My friends would describe me as ..." sentences. How dumb do you have to be to write that? They are your friends for a reason. They like you. Much better to tell me what people who think you're a slutty cow have to say. That way at least I would get a more balanced view.

I have a particularly strong level of disgust for profiles that include the following sort of crap: "I love rock climbing, sheep tossing and flying light aircraft, but am equally as happy at home with a bottle of wine and a DVD." This translates as: "I am so desperate to find a man that I will say I like anything in the hope that you will like me enough to take me out on a date." I applaud people who take the time to point out what they don't like as well as what they do. It helps me to make an informed decision. So many female dating profiles mention bottles of wine and DVDs. OK I get it. You girls like films and wine. I like wanking in the shower, chilli con carne, skimmed milk, and I'm a Celebrity Get Me Out of Here. None of these requires a mention in my dating profile.

One of the perennial challenges facing online daters of a certain age is the issue of children. My sampling of women in my target age group reveals that there are few that either do not have or do not want children. If I were to eliminate these women from my search criteria I would be left with too few women for someone with my limited looks to pick from. It would pretty much guarantee to keep me single.

Even women who say they don't want children must be treated with a degree of suspicion. Scientists could no doubt explain the biology but there is a definite pro-childbirth chemical shift for many women once they find themselves in a stable relationship. I like to believe that if I met someone I truly loved who really wanted kids my plans would change to accommodate them. In reality, after my experience with Rachel, I find that as soon as the subject comes up my ardour is dampened and my enthusiasm for the relationship goes out of the window. If it comes up on a first meeting (the stereotypical late 30s female desperate for a sperm donor does exist) it guarantees that I will not be phoning the woman back.

As soon as I started going on dates, I recognised the potential for wasting a huge amount of time and, more crucially, a truckload of cash. I needed some operating principles to work to. A date with the charming Mel was to provide me with the first.

After a brief chat online, it was at Mel's suggestion that we met. I went along with it. Her profile ticked a lot of boxes and there were plenty of pictures, all of them in the same pose wearing different dresses (in retrospect, as I write this, the warning signs were there to see). She was attractive, had a decent job, no children and lived locally.

We met for a drink in a bar in Virginia Water. It went well at first. I like people to take care of their appearance but she clearly had an obsession about how she looked. She was proud of spending £150 on a haircut and £400 plus on dresses and was keen to tell me about it. She went on to inform me that she had dated a famous cricketer but that it hadn't worked out. She mentioned his name but as I know fuck all about cricket and care even less, it went over my head, something which visibly annoyed her. I started getting the distinct impression that she was more interested in how a man would look next to her than the type of person he was.

I was curious, and delved deeper into what Mel was looking for. At that, I felt her start warming to me. Underneath her wavy blonde hair, nice tits and expensive outfit I sensed her confidence was a little shaky, and that she was lonely. But just as she started to relax into the conversation, she seemed to catch herself and snapped out of it. What she said next was to prove pivotal to how I went about online dating in the future: "Well it's all just a numbers game anyway. If you go on enough dates you will find someone you like."

On average, Mel said, she went out on dates four nights a week. I told her that I would hate to live my life that way, spending hours in bars with people I didn't want to be with on the off-chance of finding someone that I did. Was there nothing else to life except the relentless search for "the one"?

I thought there was a nice person underneath all the layers of crap Mel used to protect herself so when we parted company I offered to take her out again. She said she would like to see me again and we agreed to talk the following day. By the time I had reached home she had texted to say that she had thought about it and decided she didn't think we would be very suitable together. Ahhhhhh, I thought to myself. It was an 'on reflection text', or an ORT, as my friend Billy and I would come to refer to them. Rather than be honest with someone they don't like, most people prefer to sit and smile through a date and even agree to a second. It is much safer to drop someone by text when you are out of range of their response. In the case of Mel, I was not overly bothered as I had sensed there was something of the bunny boiler about her, so I texted her back, saying, "Fair enough. I wasn't completely sure we'd be right together either. Hope you find the person you're looking for." Then I went to bed. A "sweet" text from her was waiting for me when I awoke: "You only said that because I dumped you first."

Bless her.

Mel taught me two big lessons. I didn't want to bankrupt myself with four dates a week, nor did I want to become addicted to dating. I, decided it was safer to chat to one woman online at a time. (In any case, it felt like a betrayal to be having conversations about a potential relationship with more than one person). Somewhere deep in my psyche my father must have planted some code that means I still get embarrassed at the idea of splitting a bill. In my twenties, I had limited cash with which to indulge my interest in girls. As a result it became necessary to limit my financial risk in the event of relationships failing to blossom. Stock market traders use a similar tool, called a "stop loss limit", to restrict their losses on market trades, something I will refer to as "SLL". When a stock falls to the stop loss limit it is immediately sold, thus limiting the exposure of the trader. I used a similar strategy for women. The basic principle was this: I invested an SLL of up to and including £100 on dating any one lady. This value could be a single evening out, or spread over a series of events (there was no time limit). If by the time the £100 value was reached I had not had the opportunity to sleep with her, the stop loss triggered and I stopped seeing her. (For the record, my career average was around £75 and my personal best was £6.50.)

Although after the split with Michelle I was in a much stronger financial position than in my twenties, it was still no excuse for failing to keep a close eye on the dating budget. I maintained a rough track of my cost per date with the aim of keeping myself on the right side of prudence. What I found was that it was easy to control at an early stage, but once I liked someone my budget tended to go out of the window and the costs could rapidly accelerate.

Anette was my first successful incursion into online dating. By that I mean she was the first girl I was with for a period greater than a week. She was bright blonde with a quirky personality, a good bank balance and huge eyelashes which I presumed she applied as a deliberate statement of non-conformity. To her credit she always paid her way but I soon noticed that the costs were rising. Even when I'd thought we had settled on what was her idea of a cheap date, meeting for a drink at a local hotel, our four glasses of wine on a Saturday afternoon ended up costing us eighty-eight pounds. After this, I began to construct a new dating plan in my mind, should I need it in future.

The fact that I was aware of the mounting costs that our short relationship was incurring was probably a sign that there were doubts in my head. One small but significant thing happened on the first night Anette and I spent together. We were going at it like a pair of drunken monkeys when, in the heat of the moment, a glass of red wine was knocked off the bedside table. I stopped what I was doing and rushed out to get a cloth and some carpet stain solution (the solution failed and in the end the stain came out with table salt). It wasn't an expensive carpet or even one that I particularly liked, and later I figured that if I had been in love, the implications of the wine stain would have waited until morning.

The dating plan I used in my less flush twenties, prior to meeting Michelle, had been linked to the dating credit system insofar as I had skilfully budgeted for three dates that came in under the £100 SLL. Date one was a drink and some food, always at TGI Fridays. Now, in the modern world, TGI's may not seem the most sophisticated of places for a date but before judging me prematurely, you need to know that:

• This was the early 90s and the TGI brand was still reasonably new and interesting

•.I was mainly dealing with girls raised in Essex so the place was perfect for them to believe they were getting a posh night out without the anxiety that at any moment they might embarrass themselves

If TGI's was a success I would have collected a snog and maybe a quick arse feel before sealing a further date.

My choice for second dates was quirky: London Zoo. My logic here was simple: animals tend to make women soften and get all cutesy, and if the animals did not do this then there were lots of sweet children running around making noise and mess to appeal to their maternal instincts. The zoo was also an opportunity to demonstrate both my compassionate side and my knowledge of the animal kingdom. (Until now, my encyclopaedic knowledge of the natural world had done little to make me attractive to women.)

Date two usually turned out to be a resounding success, and there was always a good chance of sex straight afterwards. One of the secrets to the zoo was the implied spontaneity of the idea. It was all in the setup. I would pause, look at the sky, and then at the girl, and say, "I have just had a really fun idea. How do you fancy a day out at the zoo?" The only problem was that as I became increasingly familiar with the venue I was always in danger of getting caught out. One particularly gorgeous girl (ah, Hayley, where are you now) looked at me quizzically and said, "You seem to know your way around here really well." I was about to be outed when the most astonishing idea formed in my mind. I grabbed her hand, stared intently into her eyes, and said, "Do you know what? I think you're right. It must be childhood memories of being here." Needless to say, those words emotionally broke her and we went on to have a fun few weeks together before she dumped me.

The third date was always at my house where I would cook for the lucky lady. Again I felt this demonstrated a couple of key points: namely that I had my own place and that I could cook. I did indeed have my own place and I could indeed cook … the precise dish I made for this date. I'd found the recipe for Pineapple Chicken with Noodles in a men's magazine and it impressed me with its simplicity, cheapness, flavour and appearance. Looking back, I can now see that it was not that impressive, but relative to what most guys could achieve in the kitchen I'd figured it put me ahead by a mile.

My first dating plan was fairly successful in its day but, with the benefit of hindsight and an additional twenty years' experience, I could see it needed upgrading for the new millennium.

Selecting dates can be a minefield with women being so fickle about diet, terrified about being seen eating in front of someone, how they look in daylight, and on and on. The revised plan I used as my default started off with an evening drink (I was to later revise this to a mid-morning coffee so as to limit the number of evenings I wasted). In cases where I felt particularly warm towards someone or had already met them, I might choose lunch as the first date. Provided we got through this, and there were no ORTs exchanged, I always chose dinner for the second meet. Having moved on from TGI Fridays, I always asked my date if she had a restaurant she enjoyed. This covered me in the event that the meal was awful. If I had to choose, I had a list of four from which to pick.

There is something so intimate about staring at each other across a candlelit table and eating together. Having said that, I have to concentrate very hard when eating in front of strange women. I have a tendency to speed-eat and take unnecessary risks with fork loading. It is rare for me to make it through a meal without at least one spill, something you can get away with when you're younger, say five. It is not so endearing to females when you are an adult.

The day out date has been upgraded but because I've relegated it to a later date in the dating timetable I rarely get to do it anymore. The saddest thing is that I have never been on holiday with a woman since Rachel, although weekends away have been achieved on several occasions. The timing of a request to go away for a weekend is crucial and requires skilful reading of the progress you have made. Suggesting a weekend away cannot help sounding like: "Fancy coming away so I can have sex with you?" so I prefer to do it after I have slept with them, to avoid embarrassment.

The home cooking date is still right up there at the pinnacle of my dating strategies, but you will be pleased to know that I have significantly extended my repertoire. The break-up with Michelle had been the end of one of the country's great dinner-party couples, as she had been masterful in the kitchen and I was a convivial host and drinks-maker. One priority that came as result of our split was to acquire better cooking skills, and now, through practice, I have become rather good at it.

Women love to sit and watch a man cook. On occasion, I am sure I saw a woman's underwear evaporate as I chopped fresh ingredients in front of her and for this purpose I swiftly purchased two nice stools for my breakfast bar so my date could sit and watch. Pineapple Chicken, which has not appeared once on the menu in the last five years, has been replaced by a spectrum of interesting oriental and western meals. I am not about to miss out on a relationship for lack of culinary skills.

Before I fully open my dating kimono for your detailed inspection there is one question that I am often asked (mostly by men, to be fair). How many dates should happen before a couple sleeps together? The issue was a minefield in my younger days when my raging hormones did battle with my shyness. To my mind there is no right or wrong answer but I have found that almost every woman who was going to sleep with me did so after the second date. There have been a few who have held out until up to

THE HILARIOUS TRUE ACCOUNT OF A SINGLE MAN'S SEARCH FOR LOVE

five dates have passed, but that is unusual. I don't know how this compares to other men, but I am not in the slightest bit pushy about sex with women, and am generally embarrassed to bring the subject up. It is a statistic of which I am neither proud nor ashamed. It is laid before you for your information only as we delve into the murky waters of online dating and beyond.

My final online dating profile
- *Sagittarius •*
- *5'9" / 175 cm •*
- *Male •*
- *White/Caucasian •*
- *Average Build •*
- *Divorced •*
- *No children •*
- *Atheist •*
- *Doesn't smoke •*
- *Drinks socially*

STORY

Hello :) I am a happy go lucky fella who splits my time between Hampshire where I have my own business and Essex where my family and friends live.

I am high energy and believe in having fun at whatever it is I am doing. I work as a business coach which means I am highly tuned into people (but don't worry I leave the coaching at the door when it comes to relationships).

When I am not working, at the gym or relaxing I like reading, cooking, snowboarding and pretty much trying anything. My fave nights out are going to see live music, comedy, eating, drinking. Love hanging out (not literally) in London but also escaping to the countryside and the coast.

Jesus I am exhausted reading that lol. Would love to speak to you if any of the above floats your boat :)

PERFECT MATCH

If you are fun-loving, sociable, friendly tactile, impulsive and happy-go-lucky then we are going to fall in love and probably go on to change the world.

PERFECT DATE

Best date I ever had (so far) was at a London zoo evening opening. All my favourite ingredients were there - animals, beer, music, barbecue food and people who were chilled and having fun. It pissed down with rain unfortunately so can only imagine how great it would have been in sunshine :)

However why don't we start with a glass of wine somewhere quiet and find out about each other?

MUSIC

Lots of stuff. Too much to list here. Love music and would give up vital organs before I surrendered my iPod. From James Blunt to Gary Numan and all flavours in between.

All attempts to be cultured have been epic fails. So while you enjoy ballet, opera and musicals with your friends I will be in the pub waiting for you.

MOVIES

The Shawshank Redemption, Anchor Man, Borat, Predator, As Good as it Gets, the Bucket List. Watch anything once and love going to the cinema but I am very protective of my popcorn.

BOOKS

I read a book every week for my work so you will find me full of opinions and quotes. I love inspirational ideas and stories. My desert island book would be "A short history of nearly everything" by Bill Bryson

The recipe for Pineapple Chicken can be found at www.tidyuponyourwayout.com along with some stories that never made the book.

The Near Miss

One night I was at one of Paul's gigs standing on my own, as the only friends I had there were the band. Not wanting to look too much of a Billy-no-mates, I scanned the bar and caught the eye of some girls who looked like they might not throw their drinks over me if I went to talk to them. I always find cold approaches challenging, but on this occasion the idea of a night on my own pushed me through my comfort zone and off I went.

That's how I met Mary.Although her friend looked as if she'd stab me if I so much as talked to her, Mary seemed happy in my company and talked freely. She came from Dagenham, had grown up children, and was considering going back to college. With her short blond bob and steady blue eyes there was something refreshingly straightforward about her, so I struck while the iron was hot (and while I was still in Essex) and invited her to come out for Sunday lunch with me the next day.

The Sunday lunch is a massively under-utilised dating resource. I have learned to love it, primarily because I love roast dinners and figure that if I end up eating one with someone who is dull, at least I still get the roast. In this case, I liked Mary and the lunch. It wasn't totally perfect, but although the bonfire of love might not have been fully burning there was definitely a pilot light.

The whole distance thing still troubled me but I decided not to sweat about it at this stage and a week later I drove the familiar hour and a half, eighty mile journey round the M25 to Essex. This time we had dinner before going to the cinema. Again it was a nice evening, but as I drove the eighty miles back home I knew that my head wasn't in quite the right place. I was having a bad time at work and this was contributing to my unsettled feeling. I hated the company I was working for and didn't much like my colleagues, and I was feeling stressed to the point of illness. I knew I was becoming increasingly less effective, and as there was nowhere to hide in my senior position, I needed to plan my escape route.

The idea of moving to another corporation was not making me feel any better, so I had begun to think about working for myself. I had been paid a regular monthly salary ever since I left school at sixteen and the thought of giving that up and starting my own business was exciting and scary in equal measure. Against this backdrop, I decided not to worry about where the relationship with Mary was going. I figured that this was the one area of my life where I could just have some fun and not take myself so seriously, and provided I did not make any promises that I was not able to keep, it would be okay to carry on. Looking back, I should have shared this information with Mary, but at the time I was too distracted by my work to give it proper thought.

We fell into the alternate weekend pattern, familiar to anyone dating women with children. Mary was able to drive, thank God, and a lot faster than me judging from her journey times. Things bounced along nicely but I realised with some unease that her feelings for me were growing at a rate that I was not able to reciprocate.

At this point, my attention started to drift and I began to pay attention to the messages arriving from dating sites, which was a violation of one of my most fundamental values and something of which I wasn't proud. The idea that at any moment someone "perfect" may make contact is an intriguing one, even when you are seeing someone else. Scanning through profiles, in much the same way you press and squeeze vegetables in a supermarket, is a particularly addictive pastime, and it was during one such session that I briefly looked at Catherine's profile. She was pretty and young, not normally a strong combination for me, but I gave her a casual wink for good measure.

A couple of days later she wrote back thanking me for the wink and saying how much she liked my profile. This immediately made me suspicious. Early on, I had learned an important lesson about online dating. If a woman is good looking and she replies or winks at me, the odds are massively in favour of her being Eastern European. This shouldn't present me with a problem but I had heard enough examples of cultural differences getting in the way and I seemed to find dating challenging enough without any added complications. Catherine didn't sound like an Eastern European name so we exchanged a few emails and finally we spoke. Very English sounding, she was also pleasant and funny, so we agreed to meet. And that's when things started to get complicated.

After a Saturday night out with Mary, I found myself driving over to Canvey Island to meet Catherine. Although it was cold, it was sunny, which allowed me to show off my two major concessions to being middle-aged and single: my expensive sunglasses, which I had bought within two weeks of splitting up with Michelle (in my defence I didn't realise how expensive they were until I got to the counter of Vision Express and by the time £274 flashed up on the register I was too embarrassed to cancel the transaction); and my brand spanking new Audi convertible - probably one of the most obvious personifications of a mid-life crisis known to mankind. With roof down and shades and coat on, I felt good even if most people must have looked on and muttered, "tool" under their breath.

When Catherine came out to meet me I was immediately lost for words. Jesus! Long blonde hair, blue eyes, long slim legs and a perfect figure. Without question the best looking woman I had ever taken on a date. She even said I could keep the hood down, where many a woman would have been picky about their hair. This was awesome. If nothing else happened with Catherine, I would remember the feeling of driving an open-top car with an absolute scorcher sitting next to me forever. She was the ultimate optional extra for a car like this. Hunger was the only thing that stopped me taking her on a driving tour of every one of my Essex haunts on the off-chance that friends might catch sight of her in the car with me.

I had booked a table at the Boatyard restaurant in Leigh on Sea. It was a bit over the top for a "date one"; more suitable for a second or third. If Catherine had turned out to be a "for fuck's sake" at first sight I would have felt aggrieved that I was about to be robbed of my SLL in one sitting. However, although the setting was perfect, I didn't seem to be getting anywhere with her. I tried to maintain conversation and enthusiasm but got the distinct impression that she wasn't into me and that I was punching well above my weight. By the time we reached dessert it felt like I was up against the ropes. I suggested the possibility of a second date during the meal but got a lukewarm response.

Pulling up outside her house, I was surprised when Catherine asked me in for a coffee. I was even more surprised when, once we were ensconced on the settee, she reached over and kissed me. Not on the forehead or the cheek, but a direct shot to the mouth. In my head I calculated her alcohol consumption and figured she was still pretty sober. Then she said, "I wanted to do that all through lunch."

Never had I been more wrong. My legendary interpretation of body language had served me well again. It seemed that Catherine's quietness over dinner must have been because she really liked me and this had been making her feel shy. I couldn't think of any other explanation for the sudden change of behaviour. When she asked if she could come and see me the following weekend I didn't stop to consult my diary and jumped at the chance. Frankly, I would have cancelled my own knighthood for the opportunity.

There was just one problem. Mary was coming over to see a show I had booked tickets for on the Friday. Once back home, I made my mind up that it was time to end the relationship with her and I knew that having to sit through the show and dinner would be a challenge. Good fortune was on my side to some degree: Mary would have to leave to get back for her children early on the Saturday afternoon. I calculated that if I told Catherine to aim to arrive at about 3pm it would leave plenty of time to see Mary off and have a quick sweep of the apartment.

Mary came and we went to the show. I was riddled with guilt and we had a sexless night, mainly as a result of an oncoming cold starting to assault my senses. The next morning I felt like shit in spite of all the cold remedies I had swallowed. It was not the best time to talk about where we were in our relationship. I had persuaded myself that Mary was well aware that our affair had run its course but it was a colossal misread on my part. What followed was a prolonged, and sometimes loud, tirade. We were out on a walk and as it was threatening to become a real scene I suggested we went back home, had some coffee, and talked things through.

We talked and talked and talked. Or rather she did. I had put my cards on the table quickly and succinctly, and Mary clearly saw this as her turn. She lacked the brevity and clarity of my conclusion.

Meanwhile, Catherine had texted to say that she had left and told me to keep an eye out for a blue Ford Fiesta. The journey time from Canvey Island was anything between an hour and a half and two hours on a normal day. I figured it would be fine and I responded with a text giving her the gate code to get into the courtyard and told her I couldn't wait to see her.

Mary talked some more, and as time ticked by it drifted towards 2pm. We were eating into my transition time. At 2.15pm the worst of the tirade was abating and she got up and started to gather her things together. While she was in the bathroom I looked out of the window and the blood instantly drained from my face. A Blue Ford Fiesta was pulling up to the gates. Fuck! Catherine had achieved the worst case scenario journey time.

As I stood looking out of the window, Mary came and stood beside me. She said that we should talk in the week and see where things were between us after we'd had some space. I could see the gates beginning to open and the Fiesta moving forwards, before turning left and pulling to a stop in one of the visitor spaces. I was all out of ideas. The game was up.

Mary stepped through the door and I felt time slow down. I glanced over at the Fiesta. The car door opened and a tall dark haired man got out. I let out a shriek, in a very feminine way, and it even made Mary stop and ask me if I was okay.

"I'm fine," I said, but my heart was racing. I can't have looked in a good mental state. "Just thinking about what you said. Let's talk in the week."

I accompanied Mary to her car and kissed her goodbye. As she drove towards the gates, I waved and turned to go back into the apartment. Looking back one last time to check that she really had left, I saw her car moving over to allow a blue Ford Fiesta into the courtyard.

In that instant, I learned that I am not built to deal with the stress of being with more than one person at a time. The risks far outweigh the benefits.

"Who was that?" asked Catherine as she got out of her car.

"The cleaner" I answered, quick as a flash. "She just popped round to collect her money."

Catherine put her arms around me and gave me a kiss. "She looked nice."

I picked up her bag and led her inside.

I took Catherine for a walk along the High Street. I had never seen anything like it. Men were quite literally stopping in their tracks to stare at her. There were even women who looked like they would give it a go, given half a chance. It was a proud moment when I put an arm around her and felt her squeeze into me. I was sure I heard a thousand mutterings of "lucky bastard" on the wind.

Later, we drunkenly staggered to bed after having cracked open some champagne. As she stripped off, Catherine told me she had brought me a present. She'd had her private parts fully shaved in a style I believe is referred to as the "Bald Eagle". It was the first time I had seen one and I was impressed at the thoughtfulness of the gift. She had mentioned during the week that she was going to bring me something and I had been expecting a photograph of her (dressed) or maybe a packet of Revels at best. This took the idea of present giving to an instant new height, although I was concerned at how I might be expected to reciprocate.

There was another, less welcome, first for me when, to my horror, things didn't move into position as I might have expected at this stage of the proceedings. The combination of stress, champagne and cold remedies had left me as limp as a drag queen's wrist. Catherine's expression went from warm smiley anticipation to bemusement before settling on disappointed-with-just-a-hint-of-annoyed. In true female form she asked if she had done anything wrong and I spent the rest of the day assuring her that it was me not her.

After that, the romantic tone of the afternoon was pretty much destroyed. That evening, as we headed to bed for the second time, the potent trio had still not released their hold on my manhood and I could sense Catherine's crushing disappointment. At around 3am, however, the performance window finally opened. Luckily, it was Catherine who realised first, saving me the moral dilemma of whether or not I should wake her. I finally managed to do my duty and, with only a few minor requests from her, I put in a pretty good performance. (I know I should be grateful for free bedroom coaching, but I am fairly sure that every woman I have slept with has gone about seeking pleasure from our interactions in quite different ways, so advice is only ever useful in the context of that particular person.)

The following weekend, I took Catherine to a really nice country hotel just outside Bath. Fuck the SLL, Catherine was a keeper for sure. My already revised budget wasn't totally shot to pieces, though, as it was on a special deal (it had not escaped my notice that my desire to really impress women I liked was beginning to have an impact on my pocket so I felt prudence without sacrificing quallty was the new financial dating manifesto). Our room had been upgraded to a suite and as there was no one on earth that I would rather have got naked with on a four-poster than Catherine, that's exactly what we did. In fact that's all we did all day until it was time for dinner (when frankly I was relieved).

In the restaurant I could see the male halves of the other couples looking at Catherine whenever they could get away with it. She was attentive, smiling intently and holding my full eye contact whenever she could, and it must have been clear to everyone that she absolutely adored me. I felt happy and secure, staring at a woman who was massively out of my league but giving off all the signals that told me, and everyone else, that she was head over heels happy with her new man.

During the drive home she told me that she had been signed off work for a while because she was suffering with arthritis. She looked uncomfortable as she told me, as though she was breaking some really horrific news. I was only surprised that she hadn't mentioned it before, but it gave me an idea.

"Hey, if you're at home on your own, why don't you come and stay with me for a week? I'll have to work and do all my normal stuff but it would be great to have you round the house."

Catherine jumped at the chance and drove home on Sunday evening before coming back on Monday with a suitcase bulging with outfits so that she could dress up sexily for me at every opportunity.

This should have been the perfect scenario. I was lonely, and having her in the house could only be a positive, surely? We would be able to hang out in the gaps between the email shuffling and teleconferences my 'working from home' was comprised of. It didn't work out quite that way. Up to this point, all of our time together had been in blissful dating land where my attention was exclusively focused on Catherine. Now, all of the routines and habits I had developed were under scrutiny. The problem was that Catherine was bored whilst I was busy. I tried to spend time with her and, to be fair, she did her best to occupy herself with tidying up, making lunch and reading.

After a couple of days, Catherine said she felt as if I didn't want her around and was ignoring her. I countered by asking her what she would be doing if she was sitting at home on her own. Underneath, though, I felt that her statement had a worrying element of truth to it.

Soon I found myself getting irritated at every small disruption that comes with having to adapt to someone else being around. Instead of reminding myself that I had a beautiful woman I really liked all to myself, who clearly adored me, I focused on every little disturbance, every cup put in the wrong place, and every little look of disappointment on her face. Inevitably, after just three days together Catherine decided to go back to Essex and as soon as she left the house I felt the immediate relief of solitude. In the back of my mind was the thought that I might be a bit too used to living on my own.

The next day I told Catherine that I didn't think things would work out between us:

"I don't know what it is but I'm just not as attracted to you as I thought I was."

She wasn't best pleased. In fact, she went mad. I kept quiet and soaked it up when she accused me of just dating her for the sex and being a complete shit. After I had put down the receiver I spent the rest of the day pondering one simple question: "What the fuck did I just do?" What did I mean it wouldn't work? She was drop-dead gorgeous, a really nice person and head over heels besotted with me. But the damage was done. I had managed to think myself out of a potentially perfect relationship.

What didn't change, however, was that whenever I thought of Catherine all I could think about were the interruptions, her stuff all over the apartment, waiting for her to finish in the bathroom, the noise of the hairdryer … all the trivial things that most people wouldn't even notice. If I was going to be this picky over small details, finding someone to have a long-lasting relationship with was not going to be easy.

Part of me knew that in deceiving Catherine and Mary I hadn't helped the relationship. Starting out with a lie never gives a solid enough base on which to build something good. It was one of the reasons I was strongly opposed to affairs involving married people or people in committed relationships. Throughout my period of dating I had so far resisted the temptation to get involved in affairs, and on each one of the occasions I broke my own rule it had ended in disaster and there was always a part of me that had known from the start that it would.

With or Without You

After a few months I really felt I was getting to grips with the world of internet dating. Immersed in this seemingly chaotic and frantic world, patterns were beginning to emerge, and if I could only decipher them I knew I would save myself heartache, time and expense. I identified one such pattern very early on: attractive women never, ever initiate interest in me. They don't 'wink', 'flirt', 'favourite', or send me a message, which in turn places an obligation on me to ensure I keep up a high level of activity. My Saturday morning dating site raids became a standard feature of my weekends. I would make coffee, sit at my desk, and work my way methodically through online profiles. If a woman looked like a strong fit she would get a personal message and a "wink". If she was in my "not sure" group she would get a generic message (that cleverly didn't look like a generic one) and a "wink" for good measure.

One morning, I was working my way through profiles when a small pop up notification told me that Charlotte had winked at me. I immediately assumed that she would be over fifty and look like Pauline Quirke, and even when I saw her profile picture, which was really attractive, I was still doubtful. (By now I was wise to the fallibility of photographs on dating sites.) Then I read her profile.

Charlotte was thirty-four years old and lived in Craigavon, the name of which didn't ring a bell so I assumed it was up North. In any case, she was too pretty to ignore, irrespective of location. My mind went through possible scenarios: she must be looking on behalf of an ugly friend; it was a fake picture; she was a scam and I'd get an email asking for my bank account details. I sent Charlotte a message, casually asking her where Craigavon was, and then went out for the evening.

The next day she replied with a really sweet message in which, I was pleased to see, her spelling didn't look suspiciously flawed. However, her message did deliver one kick in the bollocks: it turned out that Craigavon was in Northern Ireland. As a rule, I don't mind distance in a relationship provided the journey is overland, but as soon as travel becomes marine or aeronautical, costs and complications mount up. This was going to knock my SLL straight out of the park.

Normally the conversation would have been terminated at this point but there was something about Charlotte that drew me to her. As we continued to message each other I slowly started building up a picture of her life. She had two children, one practically an adult and the other nine. She worked in security at live shows, which involved travelling across Ireland and occasionally to the mainland. She had had a problematic relationship with her children's father (a fairly consistent theme in the middle-aged dating world). Common sense should have dictated that I fold the conversation at that point, however we decided to have a chat on the phone. That clinched it for me. I was mesmerized by Charlotte's soft Irish accent, only occasionally interrupted by a slightly harsher Ulster tone, and wanted to listen to her for hours.

Charlotte sent me some more pictures. She had classic Irish looks, a kind smile and stunning deep blue eyes. Over the weeks our friendship progressed, as did the raciness of the pictures. I was at the Farnborough Airshow the day she texted me a picture of her boobs, watching the new double-decker Airbus taxi out for its first ever airshow appearance. Having always been a lover of anything to do with aviation, this was a big moment, but it was certainly made bigger by the image of Charlotte's breasts. Unsure how to reciprocate, I sent her an arty shot of a Spitfire.

A few weeks passed and we spoke most evenings as we lay in bed. It was a strange sensation to have such strong feelings for someone that you have never looked in the eye but every sense I possessed told me it was the right thing to do. Finally it came to the point where I knew that I had to see her.

There was a big smile on my face as I walked out of the arrivals area at Belfast International Airport into bright sunshine. I boarded a bus to the city centre and, as I sat watching the streets whizz by, I was struck how similar to home and yet how different the place felt. Belfast was full of attractive women. I was used to the inquisitive friendliness of the Irish, which in the past I had been known to mistake as an indication that they liked me more than they actually did. Today, though, I seemed to be attracting a lot of attention. Wearing my very favourite military coat, new jeans and tan shoes, I must have looked like a mover and shaker amongst the largely scruffy collection of urban Irish males.

From Belfast I had to catch a train out to Portadown where Charlotte worked. As soon as I reached the station I dived into the toilets, popped in my contact lenses and topped up the old Hugo Boss cologne before heading to the ticket office. It was there that I noticed that not only were the ladies checking me out but, more disturbingly, so were the men, who were watching me with a curious look on their faces.

I sat down on a bench. The buoyant feeling I'd had earlier, from being on an adventure, had twisted into a different sort of adrenalin surge. It occurred to me that there was another reason people might seem fascinated with me. I was about as English as an Englishman could be and was about to board a train heading for the so-called murder triangle. And whilst I knew that the troubles had largely subsided, it didn't stop my childhood memories of bombings and shootings on the news coming rushing back. I sensed that people in Central Belfast were largely acclimatized to English tourists, but the looks from my fellow passengers as I boarded the train suggested that the suburbs were not quite so up to speed with the idea.

Portadown, although surrounded by beautiful countryside, was a gloomy town that felt heavy with problems. By now, I had become acutely aware of my accent and decided on a policy of not asking anyone for directions, relying instead on my innate wisdom. Given that I had already spent my entire SLL on a day trip to visit someone I had never met, who couldn't spare more than an hour or two off work to see me, you would be forgiven for asking if this was a particularly useful resource for me to draw on.

If someone had sat me down with a piece of paper and asked me to describe my perfect woman I would have written down everything about Charlotte. She had black long hair, stunning ice-cool blue eyes, and when she smiled her whole face lit up. She was casually dressed and I could see that she had a perfect figure, parts of which I recognized from the airshow. Tight jeans clung to her perfectly formed bum like a spray tan. She was visibly nervous on greeting me and an awkward few minutes ensued while we both tried to figure out what to say. I was lost for words, which is rare for me, and I worried that Charlotte's quietness was caused by a disappointment that I had not lived up to what she had been hoping for.

We sat in a tiny office at the back of the furniture shop where she worked. The tight confines suited me just fine: I figured at least the journey would result in some close proximity even if not intentional. Charlotte made tea while I regaled her with the most boring travel story imaginable. There was nothing exciting to be said for flying to Northern Ireland and getting a bus and a train, and I didn't know her well enough to discuss the issues around my nationality. I knew what I wanted to say but was paralyzed with the fear that I would be rejected.

Then something surprising happened. We kissed. I had reached over to get my tea and, almost by accident, our lips met. I felt Charlotte relax. As kisses go, this one went on to break some records and we spent much of the rest of the day setting new personal bests.

When we came up for air, we headed for lunch at a local café. It felt like a friendly enough place provided you weren't me, but now I was with the most beautiful girl I had ever had the good fortune to share a fairly average cheese and pickle sandwich with I didn't give a damn. The afternoon flashed past in a haze of kissing and cuddling. We were like teenagers who had just realized that this new pastime was available to them.

Just at the stage things were starting to get almost unbearably uncomfortable physically, we had to make our tearful goodbyes. I had to limp the first few hundred yards to the station, holding a bag to cover my crotch, a problem that quickly evaporated once the oppressive atmosphere closed in on me again.

On the train back to Belfast I was torn between feelings of elation that Charlotte was everything I had hoped for and nagging doubts that this was not going to be workable. I decided to take the natural course of action and ignore them. The details and consequences could be dealt with later: at this moment I was in love.

A couple of weeks passed before I was able to get back to Belfast. In the meantime we texted and Skyped and both got more and more smitten and frustrated.

On my next visit, Charlotte didn't have to work so we hung out in a hotel bar on the edge of town. It was clear, as we sat kissing and cuddling, that the sexual tension was reaching meltdown temperature. I wanted to bring up the idea of taking a room, but the shy schoolboy in me came out and we just sat staring at each other, chatting and kissing for an hour, while I tried to think of a way to raise the idea. In the end, frustration got the better of me and I broached the subject. She readily agreed.

Approaching the reception desk, I had a sense that everyone in the place was looking at me knowingly. The receptionist was a fierce-looking woman in her fifties and I felt my face getting hotter and redder as I sensed her reading all the clues. No bags, dishevelled hair and clothes, and a beautiful woman in the bar looking at me longingly. Instead of looking disapproving, though, she played along to help me out.

"Checkout is at eleven. Would you like an alarm call in the morning?"

I could have kissed her for that, but instead asked for a 7am call. As I took Charlotte's hand, I wondered whether other men feel similarly affected by everyone knowing what they are off to do.

The room was comfortable with sunshine flooding through the net curtains, not the seedy little sex den I had envisioned. We kissed passionately and I used my best possible James Bond move to unhook Charlotte's bra and liberate her breasts. She had an amazing body, not purely because of its elegant shape and curves, but because of the way it moved as we kissed. It felt incredible to finally be in her arms.

Time slipped away and then all too quickly ran out on us. I figured that I must stink of sex and didn't want to add another reason for people to stare at me on the journey home, so I jumped in the shower. Later, at the station, as Charlotte waved to me from the taxi that would drive her home, I felt full of the calm happiness that comes with being in love and having your feelings reciprocated. Little did I know that this would be the last time I saw her.

So what happened? There was a lot going on in our lives and we lived a plane ride away from each other. I had jacked in my job and was at home planning my new work venture, as well as a holiday. (I had booked the trip of a lifetime to the Galapagos Islands as a reward for doing fuck-all for a few months.) Charlotte's neighbour and friend had suddenly died leaving a young child, and the grief and extra weight of responsibility must have been horrendous for her. I had been preoccupied in the final few days before leaving on holiday and maybe I didn't offer enough of the right kind of support. The tone of Charlotte's communications shifted and her calls and texts became less frequent. Hours of time were wasted as I racked my brains about what I might have done or said that had resulted in this gradual fadeout. My attempts to be supportive from hundreds of miles away must have come across as needy and desperate at a time when she wanted space.

The inevitable ORT arrived from Charlotte while I was on a Galapagos beach watching sea lions playing in the surf. Being in such a beautiful and wild place had a calming effect on me. I recognized that Charlotte had her own life, and the responsibility of kids, and there was no use pretending that I was going to be of any use to her or that somehow everything would resolve itself into a happy ending. Inside, I had known this moment would come from the first time I saw her, and yet still I let myself fall quickly and deeply. I sent her a note and a silver necklace from the islands.

More recently, I found Charlotte on Facebook and we have struck up a conversation and a friendship. I have begun to understand more about her. Although she is engaged now there is not a day in my life when I do not wonder about her.

She still wears the necklace.

Hot Fuzz

It took a month for me to move on from what had happened with Charlotte. There is something about unresolved relationships and feelings that have a habit of lingering in my head, way beyond their useful life. When I finally went back to look at a dating site it was a half-hearted effort. No-one was really catching my attention and those who did were not responding. What had at first seemed like a deluge of single women was now feeling more like a dripping tap.

One such drip was Karen, who was kind enough to respond to a message I sent her. She seemed friendly, lived locally, and was at least worth a few hours of time to find out more. We met at a local pub that is an old mill house with a garden that skirts round the river. I knew at once that I wasn't particularly attracted to her and was pretty sure the feeling was mutual. She was blonde with an attractive face, but she was one of those women you realise is quite prepared to stretch the words "average build" to the outer edge of their definition.

At this point, I was not in a position to start throwing stones about people's weight. After I split with Michelle, the emotional strain had the welcome benefit of helping me drop a stone with minimal effort, and within a month of breaking up I was looking in much better physical shape than I had for years. However, without the discipline of going to work every day, I had by now neutralised the bereavement dividend and was physically nowhere near where I wanted to be.

At first, my conversation with Karen was stilted and was made all the more challenging by her being decidedly cagey about one of the more obvious first date questions: "So what do you do for a living?" In the end, she invited me to guess, a game that was fun for a while, but I knew that unless the answer turned out to be fellatio teacher or a lap dancer I was likely to be underwhelmed by the answer. The clue that finally gave it away came when she said that her job put a lot of men off. I guessed immediately.

"So how long have you been in the police force?"

Karen seemed surprised at my lack of concern, and in truth her job really did not bother me. Now that we had actually found a conversation we could get stuck into I was beginning to warm to her, although she didn't give away any of the juicy stories about life in the force that were really the only thing I wanted to know about. She was surprised by my knowledge of the profession and I noticed a glimmer of warmth when I regaled her with my story of captaining the Panda Competition team at my junior school. This annual competition, sponsored by The Metropolitan Police, pitted teams from local schools against each other in a quiz about the police force, police methods, and the highway code. It had never occurred to me at the time that this knowledge would prove valuable in the wife hunt.

When I got home I was undecided as to whether to take the relationship further, so I slept on it. The next day I texted Karen and asked if she fancied going out for dinner later in the week. She seemed a little surprised, not having thought I was interested. This time we visited a restaurant in the beautiful market town of Farnham but although our date was much more relaxed and we got on well, I was still not particularly attracted to her.

My charm and slight distance must have worked because she came back to my apartment. I was pleased that earlier in the day I had undertaken a comprehensive inventory, sweep, and clearance of the apartment for anything I possessed that was of "suspect origin". We had coffee and she ended up staying the night. It was an unremarkable and not unenjoyable experience although Karen had a weird habit of laughing in the heat of the moment. This. That was really off-putting. As she didn't seem to be looking at my genitalia whilst she did so, I dismissed the habit as some kind of nervous tic.

We started to see each other a few times a week and her enthusiasm for me quickly began to outpace my feelings for her. She even drove eighty-three miles to Bath while I was on a management course, and although I was still not feeling a fire in my belly, it did allow me to learn more of her story. Alarm bells started to ring when she told me, venom leaking from her voice, that not only had she recently split up from her husband (always a confusing time of mixed emotions and shit flying around) but that the marriage had only lasted a month. I wasn't surprised to hear that her ex was also in the police, as I imagine the stresses of the job are hard to understand for an outsider. And, to be honest, it is just not comfortable hanging around with the "old bill". It is quite impossible not to feel a heightened degree of anxiety in a cop's presence, a feeling that is not surprising considering that my previous interactions with members of the constabulary had been limited to defending my incessant desire to break maximum speed limits. Being around them always makes me feel guilty even if I haven't done anything.

Over the coming weeks I was required to spend increasing amounts of time in the company of Karen's colleagues. Socialising with them, I always felt like an outsider; it always seemed as if there was an in-joke that I wasn't allowed to be part of. Her male colleagues were particularly hostile towards me. Perhaps they objected to having their harem infiltrated by a civilian.

I was about to look for an exit opportunity when one was handed to me in the strangest fashion.

My decision to brave a summit talk with Karen was driven not only by my increasing apathy towards her but also because an attractive work colleague was beginning to show some interest in me. It didn't strike me as wise to get into a "crossover" situation with someone who was likely to have excellent powers of detection and access to CCTV and call data.

The evening before I was due to meet Karen, I was driving through Camberley at what felt like a moderate speed (given my track record) when I saw a patrol car pass me, travelling in the opposite direction. I didn't feel bothered, even when I watched it do a U-turn in my rear-view mirror and accelerate to a position close behind me. I stayed resolutely focused on my speedometer, my brain going through a mental checklist of likely problems or felonies that may have been drawn to their attention. I settled on the likelihood of their having received a call instructing them to apprehend a suspect, which had led them to change direction. But then the blue lights came on and began flashing to indicate that I should pull over.

A police officer approached my car and asked me to turn off my engine and step out of the vehicle.

"Are you aware of the speed you were travelling, sir?"

Probably more aware than you are, Officer, given you were travelling in the other fuckin' direction, were the words that came to mind but that I chose not to vocalise. Instead I fumbled an answer, adding a few miles over the speed limit to demonstrate I wasn't completely naive.

"Due to the time of night, I am going to have to ask you to take a breathalyser test. Have you been drinking this evening, sir?"

At this, the Peroni and glass of white wine I'd had at dinner started to play on my mind. There was a sufficient level of doubt as to the number of units to make my sphincter tighten. As the policeman showed me the breathalyser, every episode of Police, Camera, Action I'd ever watched ran through my head as I listened to his instructions. Anxious, I botched the first attempt and he didn't get a reading. The second time I blew harder and the machine started to bleep. It was an ominous sound. The cop then showed me the reading and explained that there were traces of alcohol but not enough to put me over the limit. Although he and his fellow officer seemed quite friendly, telling me about a spate of car thefts in the area before bidding me goodnight, I could not help feeling something wasn't quite right. It was to be several hours before my heartbeat finally settled back to its normal rate.

The next evening, I met Karen as planned. As I was pouring her a glass of wine at my apartment, I jokingly said, "So what possessed you to set your friends on me last night?"

She looked quizzically at me, and as I explained what had happened her facial expression went from bemused to concerned. She asked me to describe the police officers.

Karen's face drained of all colour. "That sounds like my ex-husband."

Now it was my turn to look worried. She quickly searched through her mobile phone to find a photograph and I was able to positively identify the suspect.

"How the hell did he know who I was?" My panic was turning to anger.

Karen tried to assure me that it must be a random coincidence. "I mean, he knows I'm seeing someone, but I didn't tell him anything about you."

She told me that I shouldn't read anything into it, which was easier said than done. We spent the night together but my head was so busy analysing what had happened that I was definitely not in the mood for sex.

The next day, I told Karen I thought it was best for us to stop seeing each other. I had decided that policewomen were off territory for me.

But then came a very strange coincidence.

A few weeks later another Karen popped up on my radar screen in response to an ambitious wink on my part. (I say this because she looked pretty attractive and I was still feeling distinctly unattractive.) We chatted online and all seemed pretty promising, especially the fact that she lived only ten minutes away. Then I I found out that not only did she have the same name as my previous date but also that she was a policewoman.

As two cops on the trot, both called Karen, seemed highly implausible, I briefly considered the notion that I was somehow being framed in a sting operation by Karen number one. Then I figured that surely even the police wouldn't be quite so obvious as to send me someone with the same name.

Due to Karen number two's good looks, I weakly opted to ignore the rule I had set just a few weeks earlier and we set a midweek lunch date. I decided, given her vocation, that the stalking risk was low and suggested that she came and parked in the courtyard so that we could walk to the local pub.

When Karen stepped out of her car I became instantly self-conscious about my weight. She had the body of someone who spends loads of time in the gym and looked gorgeous. Oh fuck, I knew this feeling. We kissed on the cheek and made our way to the pub. If there had been some random road works or a new lamppost that day you can be fairly certain I would have ended up in casualty because I couldn't stop glancing at her. Over lunch I couldn't help ticking all the boxes in my head. She loved travelling (tick), liked animals (tick), was hot (tick) and had a dry sense of humour (tick).

A long lunch turned into a coffee and a kiss back at my apartment. We discussed meeting again but Karen said she needed to consult her shift rota. She left at dusk, and set off to work a night shift, keeping me and other villagers safe from old age pensioners fighting, or stray cats in trees, each a genuine danger in my dreamy village.

As I sat at home that evening, I daydreamed about a life with Karen. We would stay living in Hampshire as it was good for both our jobs, but we would travel lots. There would be no kids because neither of us appeared to want any but definitely animals, most likely dogs. She would make me want to be really successful, so my business would take off, and we would be well off. I knew this to be somewhat premature, but Karen number two was the perfect storm: that rare, yet perfect, blend of geography, good looks and personality (with just the slightest sprinkling of self-confidence issues to ensure I had a fighting chance of a relationship with her).

Karen appeared to like me too. The smile she had given me when we first met hadn't been a stifled giggle, after all, and there had been ample escape opportunities of which she had taken none. Over lunch, I'd detected the right body signals and to be fair I can't blame her. In spite of my crippling insecurity about my physical appearance, I was on form: witty and charming. I figured it would take a hard bitch indeed not to take pity on me.

Karen was working late shifts for the rest of the week so we arranged to see each other the following weekend. It was a cloud nine week. The sun seemed brighter, people friendlier, and work easier. She asked if we could meet on the Sunday evening. I took a breath and told her this would be difficult as I had a commitment to the courtyard quiz team and felt it would be inappropriate to let the side down. (The fact that I was utterly useless at general knowledge and therefore dispensable had not occurred to me, or my teammates.) She was really cool about it and suggested that she came over when I'd got back from the pub.

She actually wanted to come round and see me after the pub! Did life get any better than this? Even to me, it was obvious there was a sexual agenda and that she didn't want to sit and watch News at 10 or discuss the impact of community policing in the area. This was my first bona fide inbound bootie call, or at least as near to one as I had ever experienced.

My suspicions were confirmed. Shortly after Karen arrived we hit the sack and spent the night together, my performance only mildly impeded by my consumption of Directors bitter and curry earlier that evening. On the whole, I felt that I had represented the civilian male population very well.

When I woke up the next morning I was delighted to find Karen was still there and, more importantly, that she was even more beautiful than I had remembered. Seeing each other in the morning is a pivotal point for both parties in any relationship, although I suspect that the step change between evening and morning may be greater for women. The absence of makeup often reveals hidden characteristics (good and bad) in a woman's face, and although in recent years the explosion of men's product has perhaps shifted the balance a bit (I certainly look different with gel in my hair, my under-eye cream and moisturiser), so far I have not observed a stunned look of horror from a woman as her eyes opened, though there have definitely been pauses and curious looks until their brain confirms recognition.

As we lay in bed talking and laughing, feeling comfortable with each other (something that had been absent from my life for a while) I realised that it was time to ratchet things up and display my affection in the strongest and most memorable way possible. Time to make breakfast and break open the smoothie maker. The saying "the way to a man's heart is through his stomach" may well be true but there is also a related formula that works on women. It operates like this: the speed of access you are granted to a woman's private areas is in direct correlation with your ability to cook. My newly discovered culinary skills extended to a romantic and very tasty twist on the traditional fry-up, the builder's arse of romantic foods.

Making a fresh smoothie for someone says a lot. It demonstrates that you are willing to take the trouble to prepare something fresh for them in the morning, and it speaks of a healthy man full of vitality (even if the body isn't delivering the same message). It is the ultimate romantic gesture until you turn the fucking thing on and wake up everyone in a three mile radius. Karen loved the smoothie (I know this to be true as she remarked on it when I posted a picture of a freshly-made concoction on Facebook years later).

So here I was with my beautiful girlfriend after a night of sex. It was like a scene from a sitcom about a perfectly happy couple and I loved it. This must be what a happy marriage feels like, I thought to myself. Nothing could dampen my mood, not even the battle of cleaning the smoothie maker (a process that has often led me to consider just buying a stock of cheap ones and treating them as disposable) after she left.

Karen had agreed to go out with me to the pictures in the evening but said she needed the afternoon at home to sort out some stuff. I don't know why, but that afternoon a strange sensation came over me, an anxiety that something didn't feel right. I tried to convince myself I was panicking unnecessarily and consoled myself by going onto the dating site to read Karen's profile again, figuring that perhaps there was a clue there as to what she might like to see at the cinema. To my horror I found that she was online.

This was an impossible situation. As we had only just started seeing each other, confronting her about being online did not seem appropriate, and a challenge would, of course, lend itself to one from her: "How did you know I was online? Were you online?" The classic online daters' catch 22. Instead, I texted her to check how her day was going and asked her what she fancied seeing at the cinema that evening.

She replied quickly: "I've had a change of mind. We're not really well suited and I think we should call it a day."

I couldn't quite believe what I was reading so, just to be sure, I re-read it ten times. A horrible feeling of aching emptiness began to well in my stomach. In an instant the world felt very different. Everything was spinning, so I slumped onto the chair and did what every self-respecting guy would do. I broke down and cried. These weren't just tears for Karen, they were tears for Rachel, tears for Charlotte, and tears for my own miserable fucking state.

The rest of the day was spent replaying every action and comment as I tried to figure out why Karen had dumped me. Perhaps I had said the wrong thing, maybe I was rubbish in bed, maybe she wasn't such a big fan of fresh fruit smoothies after all. Texting her made very little difference, as I was still none the wiser about her motives, although I did get an "it's not you, it's me" message (kind-hearted-woman-code for "it's you"). There is a limit to how many texts you can send without appearing desperate or stalky and I am sure I exceeded it.

I thought I would never hear from Karen again, but then, one Monday morning several weeks later, she popped up again. Two days earlier, I had been charging around my apartment frantically packing for a weekend away. The Sunday evening, I had arrived back late and, exhausted, had dumped my bags and went straight to bed. There was nothing of note to wake up for on Monday morning so I had a lie-in.

Under normal circumstances, if there is even the faintest chance of a hot woman arriving at my apartment, it is scrubbed from top to bottom, along with me and the cat. Ordinarily, my apartment has pulling power: it is very cool. The agent who sold it to me always said it would end up being owned by a bachelor, as it oozes sophistication and sexiness. My long-held fantasy of tying a woman to my spiral staircase may not have been fulfilled at the time of writing but there is no denying that women do tend to fall in love with the place. Right now, though, it looked terrible, with clothes, towels, shoes, and bags strewn everywhere, plates in the sink, and the litter tray smelling like an elephant had used it.

At about 8.50am the doorbell rang. Rubbing the sleepers out of my eyes I pulled myself out of bed. As I made my way through the hallway I caught sight of myself in the mirror. It was not a good look. Unshaven, live plug socket hair and what I really hoped was a pasta sauce stain on my dressing gown. I could see through the glass that it was a uniformed person at the door. The postman is in for a hell of a shock, I thought, but something about the frosted silhouette didn't look right. As I got closer I could make out a police uniform and began to worry, but when I opened the door there was Karen.

Back in the old days, I had a bit of a thing about WPCs' uniforms. These days, however, a desire for utility has replaced any traces of sexiness. Karen was wearing boots, trousers, and a belt that made me think of a Star Wars stormtrooper. However, given my own physical appearance at that moment I still figured that she could beat me in a dress-off.

"Erm, Karen?" I said, whilst trying to flatten my hair.

She smiled and stepped in. "I was early for an interview with an estate agent in the High Street. Have you got time for a coffee?"

As Karen climbed the stairs, I watched her scan the scene (I was suddenly aware of my laptop in full view and worried that I didn't know its origin). She climbed over the mounds of detritus on her way to the kitchen and the embarrassing thought occurred to me that it was probably not unlike what she might encounter at the scene of a violent crime.

Her eyes took in everything. "Wow, Dave, you really took our break-up hard, didn't you?"

At that, I broke into uncontrollable laughter.

We have remained in touch since then and I still really like her. When I last heard anything, she was engaged and seemed happy.

One important thing I learned from the experience with Karen was that I had wasted a lot of energy searching for what it was that I had done wrong. Taking knocks like this to my already flaky self-confidence I knew was not going to help me, and it would be a while before I was ready to try again. I vowed that next time things would have to be different, and underneath all the hurt I felt a new sensation rising. I was beginning to feel anger at the way I had been treated.

Pretty Polly

I avoid going on dates with women that have been "recommended" by my female friends. There is a simple reason for this: women generally have terrible taste in women. As I am no psychologist, I cannot offer a technical explanation for this, but I do know that it's to do with female friend relationships being deep and emotional. So deep, in fact, that it clouds their judgement about the aesthetics of their friends. I have never been on a date with a genuinely attractive friend of a friend, but have been out with plenty of ugly ones. Not only have I had to endure these dates but I have also had to break the awkward news to a mate that their lifelong friend is a dog.

Looking at Polly's photo on Facebook, I reckoned that she was pretty much as had been described by my friend Sarah, so I decided to give it a whirl and take her to a pub on the south coast. During the drive I found her to be bright, a little quirky, very open and definitely fanciable. She told me about a couple of her more recent consorts: a rich guy who let her drive his Ferrari, and one who took her for a KFC (to be fair it was in Bath, in my view one of Britain's most beautiful and romantic cities) with his mates. As the day progressed, I noticed something in the tone of her voice that came across as a little bossy, but at this stage it was only a minor issue. I had already decided she was to be my next girlfriend.

Back at Polly's place, I was introduced to a very girlie dog and shown around her house. It was clearly suffering from a lack of male presence (she had two grown-up daughters, one of whom was a little too grown-up from the photographs). There were far too many soft furnishings, pastel colours and pink things scattered around for my taste. Her eye was equally critical of my clothes, I suspected, as she made frequent references to my style and dress sense (these could have been taken as compliments or warnings. I took them as the former).

Later, on her very fluffy sofa, Polly revealed herself to be an astonishingly good kisser and, as first kisses are a generally good indicator of the degree of energy and passion women bring to the bedroom, I felt sure that our next date was going to be something special.

My memories of that next date are limited, beyond what I can only describe as a colossal whirlwind of a bedroom performance. We went at it for hours, and Polly absolutely smashed the life out of me. There were body parts flying all over the place as we threw each other around in a frenzy of mad lovemaking. There were times where I was genuinely disorientated, not knowing where I was in relation to her face. It is interesting to note that this display of intense passion was not as a result of anything particularly special on my part. Indeed, quite the opposite. I had not had sex for a considerable period of time, rendering my initial contribution brief but spectacular - a fact that Polly was not shy in pointing out although she put it down to her own incredible sexiness whereas I knew at that point the sight of any intimate part of any females anatomy would likely have triggered a similar response. But Polly just kept on going and I found my powers of recovery to be beyond what I had previously thought physically possible.

Outside of the bedroom, I quickly realised that there was something not quite right about our personality mix. Polly asked me a string of questions about my past, and my still regular trips to Essex, which I sensed weren't born out of genuine curiosity or a desire to understand her new man. Instead, they felt like interrogations, loaded with suspicion. Feeling controlled and monitored is never a good thing for me and it usually has the effect of my withdrawing from relationships very quickly.

There was also something going on with Polly's ex (the KFC man). The last time they had seen each other she had left a pair of shoes at his flat. According to her version of events, he was now holding them hostage, attempting to use them as a bargaining tool to meet her again. This resulted in an irritating exchange of texts that continued throughout the entire time we were dating. At one point she asked me what she should do and, being a man, I presented her with an elegantly simple solution: buy a new pair of shoes and cut off all contact with him. Now, I am aware of the relationship some women have with their shoes, but in this case it seemed a simple matter of economics. The shoes were worth £50 (as new) and I figured that it would cost her more in petrol to retrieve them than to buy a new pair. When Polly chose to ignore my solution it felt clear to me that she still had a glimmer of attraction towards the guy. That this didn't bother me revealed how little I cared for her.

But there was the sex. I am not proud that I continued the relationship because of it, but at the time it felt like the right thing to do. Most of the time we stayed at my apartment, and it was on the one occasion we spent the night at hers, making love amongst a mountains of throws and cushions, that she first used her nickname for my genitalia.

When a woman has that much soft pink stuff in her house you know it is only a question of time before she nicknames your penis. However, "Little Dave" and his owner weren't happy with the

THE HILARIOUS TRUE ACCOUNT OF A SINGLE MAN'S SEARCH FOR LOVE

choice. (Although I had come up with one for her fanny, "Cavern Crotch", but had the sense to keep it from her.)

Women can be remarkably obtuse when it comes to using size-related adjectives to describe a man's penis. And even if you think that talking about your ex's small cock will make your new man feel special, I have news for you. We're not thick. We know that after the split you will refer to our appendage in a scale designed to deride us to your friends.

Christmas was fast approaching. Happily, I had already committed to a snowboarding holiday with a friend, but, as a compromise, I promised Polly that we could spend New Year's Eve together, which seemed fair. However, a chance phone call with Paul reminded me that I had already promised to spend New Year's with him. I knew I had to think through the issue carefully of how to broach this with Polly, but what I actually did was keep ignoring it, hoping it would go away.

As my relationship with Polly was not founded on a bedrock of love, or even like, I wasn't inclined to go overboard on a gift for her. We had been dating less than a month and I wasn't even sure this put us in the present buying window at all. It was not a subject I felt comfortable discussing with her, so I added it to the ignore list that was steadily growing. I am naturally programmed to avoid conflict, and when I get into arguments my lucidity of speech and clarity of thought quickly disappear. In contrast, Polly seemed to come alive in disagreement and it was a probably that trait, more than any other, that drove me to decide I really didn't like her.

I didn't want to be embarrassed if Polly presented me with a huge symbol of love in the form of a high-value present, so I came up with a plan. I bought a couple of gifts of moderate value and an iPod. I would keep the iPod aside, and only give it to her in the event she pulled out a similar high-value gift.

We celebrated Christmas together on my birthday, 20th December. In the morning, Polly gave me my birthday gift: a set of cushions for my living room (clearly she had picked up on the disproportionate amount of soft furnishings in my apartment compared to her house) and some ornaments for the house. Her choice made me suspicious that I was the subject of an experiment to see if she could make me conform to her standards of household inventory (where Pavlov used dog biscuits, she used sex). But my disappointment at receiving nothing of interest to a male was outweighed by my relief that she was not spending excessively.

After lunch, we exchanged Christmas gifts. I was pleased to find that things were balanced well, financially, so I did the benevolent thing anyway, and parted with the iPod. Polly was over the moon and it was not long before I was invited to partake in afternoon sex as a reward for being such a good boy.

Later that evening, I reflected that everything had worked out beautifully. Polly, clearly happy with the day, was inclined to talk after we'd had sex. This is a common phenomenon amongst women, and one I have trained myself to deal with by mumbling a string of stock phrases whilst being half-asleep, but this time the subject of New Year's Eve instantly pulled me out of my slumber.

Given my relative success at keeping Polly happy over the past twenty-four hours, I figured that now would be as good a time as any to confront the issue.

"Polly, I've been really stupid [truth], but my friend called me yesterday [lie], and reminded me that I had accepted an invitation to spend New Year's Eve with him and his family [truth]. I feel idiotic [truth] and upset [lie] because it means I won't be able to see you until after the New Year."

I had hoped, considering the lateness of the hour, that Polly's response might be muted. Instead, she went ballistic. My attempts to position myself as someone of high moral standing who felt that letting his friend down was against his deepest values were to no avail.

Polly countered with: "Surely he'll understand that you've met someone and after being away for a week you'd want to spend New Year with me?"

It was hard to argue this one, especially as it was late and I was still a bit dozy, but I stuck to my guns.

Then Polly threw a curve ball: "Well, why don't I come with you?"

Even in my comatose state I knew this would be crossing the line. The thought of introducing her to Paul as my girlfriend was not an idea I was ready to entertain, but I knew that if I were to say this it might provoke "neighbour-waking" levels of shouting.

"Polly, it's only been a month, and I feel it's too early to be wheeling you around my friends and family."

This led her on a whole new tack, a line of interrogation that was clearly designed to find out if I was having an Essex-based affair.

Eventually, she offered a "them or me" ultimatum which I grabbed with relief, politely telling her that she could never come between my friends and me. I even managed to look smug and virtuous as I said it.

Polly stormed out of the room, shouting that she was going home. "You're clearly only interested in sex, you bastard!"

I assured her that it was not the case [lie]. I also managed to get in the suggestion that she shouldn't drive home, as she had drunk way too much, telling her that I could sleep on the settee. I deliberately didn't suggest that she come back to bed with me, not only because I wanted to prevent my penis taking over rational control, but also in the desire to protect myself from violent attack.

Instead of agreeing to wait until morning, Polly phoned a friend who agreed to come and pick her up. As she did this, I wondered how many of my friends would leave their warm beds on a winter night to rescue me from the clutches of a mad lover.

In the hour before he finally got to my house I had to sit and soak up a barrage of abuse about my conduct as a human being and, more specifically, a male human being. It was a huge relief when finally she decided to wait for her rescuer outside.

I lay there in the darkness, too unsettled to sleep and afraid that Polly might burst back in and attack me. I felt badly about the whole thing and knew that I had proved myself utterly incapable of having a "fuck buddy" arrangement, having learned too late that it would have been only reasonable to let the other person know there was such an arrangement in place. I made a pledge that I would never date someone I had doubts about again, no matter how good the sex was.

Finally, sleep overtook me and when I woke up the next day Polly's car was gone from the courtyard. I made some tea and sat on the sofa. As I did so, a wry smile came over my face. I saw that, even in the heat of her fury, she had remembered to take the iPod.

TIDY UP ON YOUR WAY OUT

Mad Cow Disease

Jane was a slam-dunk online date. A wink, a joke about horses, and we were away. For some reason I meet a lot of single women who love horses. There are two hypotheses for this. The first is that I have some weird "opposites attract" psychology going on, because I hate horses. (An embarrassing dismount from a donkey in a holiday camp donkey derby when I was seven put paid to any idea of riding any animal that was bigger than me.) The second, more plausible, explanation is that these women spend all of their time with, only talk about, and smell like horses. As a result their husbands get bored with playing second fiddle to an animal and leave them. I'm sure this explains the exponentially growing pool of single equestrian females.

However, whilst I do not like horses, I do like women with pert bottoms and a good sense of balance, and am partial to a pair of jodhpurs and riding boots. It is also fortuitous that my donkey story has the effect of melting the hearts of lady riders who seem to have an overwhelming desire to help me past that childhood incident.

Jane seemed interesting, and after a conversation on the telephone in which she told me that she worked in the horse racing industry and travelled to race meetings all over the country and aren't horses amazing blah blah, I made arrangements to meet her for lunch the following Sunday in my local pub, the Cricketers.

She drove up from Winchester and arrived on time (an important start for someone as punctual as me). With scant disregard for my own safety I directed her to my house so that she could park in the courtyard. This was something I'd done in the past but it was, with hindsight, a dangerous move. Women are much more careful about not letting strange men know where they live;: only disclosing the information after a date or two. Being a man, I didn't think of my own safety in that way, and it seemed the only logical thing to do, as parking in the village can be a challenge.

Jane was not the worst looking woman I had wasted a few hours with, but she was definitely in the top ten. Where the attractive, slim blonde I had winked at on the dating site? It seemed that I would need carbon dating tools to establish how old the photograph she had used really was. I felt a sting of disappointment but figured that at least I had some food to look forward to, and as I was feeling particularly hungry, suggested we walked straight over to the pub. This also afforded me some protection, as I was able to avoid having to show her precisely which apartment in the block was mine.

My home village is perfect. Quintessentially English with a neat little parade of independent shops, a couple of duck-ponds and a lovely cricket green. Next to that is the pub, my regular, at which I participate in the Sunday quiz evenings. Basically this pub was as close to my home as it could be without having my underpants strewn round the floor. The small and intimate dining area has neat little two-person tables. Ordinarily, I love the cross-chatting between groups that such proximity allows, but this wasn't to be one of those days.

I led us to the bar, where I said "bonsieur" in my best Del Boy accent to the petite French lady and her husband who were serving. Jane opted for a large glass of Pinot Grigio and because I wasn't in the mood to make a decision, I had the same. We sat down at the bar and the conversation flowed easily. I was interested in her work which from what I could gather consisted of travelling to horse racing meetings and getting pissed. It seemed like a great way to make a living, if you are interested in horses and posh people. As we chatted, the Pinot Grigio was in free flow and I noticed her glass was finished by the time I was half way through mine.

I had decided, somewhere between the house and the pub, that I was not particularly attracted to Jane and was unlikely to want to see her again. Instead of feeling discomfited by this thought, it actually made for easy conversation as I didn't have to think too much about what I said. On the other hand, I was concerned that if I drank too much, she might become attractive enough for me to make a pass at, so I slowed my intake. Judging from the speed Jane was drinking, she had the opposite thought, hoping, perhaps, that if she downed enough I might become better looking.

By the time we were ready to have lunch there were subtle traces of slurring in her voice and as we walked to our table there was a definite teeter to her walk. A few feet away were a couple, in their fifties, who gave us a friendly smile as we sat down. They looked familiar, but in that village way where it is hard to know whether you've met at the butcher's or in the One Stop queue. Civility is a byword in my village, which recently won a best place to live in Britain award, and for me it is an important part of what makes it such a great place to live.

We both ordered a Sunday roast. This made perfect sense given that it was lunchtime and a Sunday. Then a bottle of Pinot Grigio arrived, and Jane wasted no time in putting it away. I am pretty sure if it had been a puddle instead of a bottle she would have got down on all fours and dropped her face in it. By the time the food arrived, she had gone beyond the tipsy classification and was in the early stages of the pissed envelope. She kept leaning in to talk to me in that conspiring way pissed people do, and the flirting notched up a gear. Fluttering her eyelashes, she started making regular excursions onto my side of the table with her hand. The table was only small and I am sure it wasn't necessary to lean over to get the horseradish sauce in quite such a cleavage-opening way. It was small relief that she didn't lick the spoon seductively afterwards.

So far, it hadn't been an unpleasant encounter. Although increasingly pissed, Jane was moderately amusing and the food was as delicious as ever. Something about the background chatter of happy people reassured me: it meant that I was not alone with her.

At first I didn't take much notice of the fact that Jane's attention had begun to focus on the couple sitting next to us. Every now and then she would pause and glance in their direction, eventually signalling with her hand for me to move closer so she could whisper something.

"That couple are fascinated by us. They're listening to our every word."

This took me aback. For one thing I hadn't noticed. For another it made me apprehensive: there was an odd, not entirely friendly, look in Jane's eye. My diplomatic skills in such situations have got me out of high risk situations in the past and I fell upon their support now.

I whispered back: "Hey Jane, I've a loud voice so I'm kind of used to people hearing what I'm saying. In any case, it's not as if we're saying anything confidential or anything. Why don't we just enjoy our meal."

For a while, my act of appeasement seemed to work and normality was restored. The conversation resumed when I asked Jane some questions about dating within the equestrian scene but the sideways glances did not stop. Suddenly, in mid conversation, Jane stopped, calmly wiped her mouth with her napkin, and turned to the people at the next table.

In her politest, posh-horsey, yet drunken, voice she addressed them: "I was wondering if you would care to join us …"

For a fleeting moment I thought it was just a nice gesture, if somewhat odd, as we had all finished eating. But every hook has its barb, and hers engaged sharply.

"… given that you seem to find our conversation so much more fascinating than yours."

The world froze. For a moment I left my own body and was floating above the scene with my hands clasped over my head. If an Al-Qaeda cell had burst into the pub, thrown a sack over me and hustled me out to a waiting car I would have kissed them. It was hard to gauge whether the lady at the next table or I was the more stunned as we sat there with our mouths ajar. My brain was calculating potential next steps at an alarming rate and once the processing slowed, I spoke:

"I must apologise for my girlfriend as she's had rather too much to drink. But please don't worry, we're leaving now."

This felt like a line from a Hollywood movie and for a brief moment I imagined how my ex-wife would have reacted if I'd had the courage to use it on her. Before Jane had a chance to react, I paid the bill, got our coats and shuffled her out of the restaurant. As I left, I gave the couple next to us a skyward roll of the eyes. This seemed to appease them. The husband even gave me a knowing look that seemed to say "Don't worry we've all been there."

As we staggered back to my apartment I had just one thing on my mind: how quickly I could get Jane to leave. Her body language told another story. She appeared to have experienced an entirely different afternoon to me. She smiled as she happily slipped her arm through mine. All my senses were on the alert, trying to choose between fight or flight. I moved with deliberate pace towards the apartment, feeling icily in control, until a thought made me suddenly freeze. Jane had arrived by car.

Jane was clearly drunker than a sailor on shore leave and her vehicle was occupying a visitor bay in the courtyard where I had allowed it, and her, to infiltrate my defences. What was I to do? I'm not one to encourage drink driving, but at the same time I didn't want her coming into my apartment or having a reason to return the next day.

I decided the latter option was preferable to the first: "Are you getting home by taxi or train?"

My avoidance of other options went straight over Jane's head and she gave me one of those "relax Dave, I really like you and am going to stay with you" looks that would normally have me sprinting for the condom drawer. She wasn't so drunk that she didn't sense my lack of enthusiasm for the idea, however, and moderated her position.

"It's okay, I'll just have some coffee and drive home when I've sobered up a bit."

This wasn't an answer I'd planned for. By my calculations, Jane was a good forty-eight hours from being sober by anyone's definition, let alone the Law's. So, as there wasn't a win-win situation available, I did what any man would do, and lied.

"Okay, I'll make you a coffee but I have to go out soon so I'm afraid you'll need to find a way to get home."

Jane didn't react to this, being more intent on relieving the considerable build-up of fluid in her system. While she made herself at home in my bathroom I wondered hopelessly if I could sit Jane down with a coffee and disappear into another room while she drank it. The trouble is that my apartment is open plan, the kitchen, dining and living areas in one space, which affords no opportunities of doing so, unless you retire to the bedroom, which was clearly not an option.

As I was pouring the coffee, Jane came up behind me, put her arms around me and kissed the back of my neck. This was so unexpected and uncomfortable that it made me shiver. I moved quickly away to get sugar, pointing the bowl at her wordlessly. She declined the invitation, took her cup, and went to sit outside on the balcony. After spending as long as I could pretending to tidy an already immaculate kitchen, I went outside. As I sat down, she leaned over to take my hand. This was it. I had run out of options.

Instead of using the ORT I had originally planned to send later that evening, I said: "We are very different people and whilst I like you [a lie born out of fear of violence] there's not going to be any relationship between us."

Jane looked genuinely stunned and stared at me as though what I had said was the maddest thing she had ever heard in her life. The adrenalin was coursing through my veins and I knew I had to kill the situation fast, so without waiting for her answer, I offered the same choice as I had delivered earlier: taxi or train. This was no time for ambiguity.

Jane avoided eye contact as she drank the rest of her coffee. Ignoring the uncomfortable static in the air, I pressed her for an answer as to her mode of transport. At that, she glared at me, picked up her bag and walked to the door.

"I'll be fine driving. I don't want to spend a minute longer here."

"Look Jane, I'm really uncomfortable with ..."

She cut me off, saying something along the lines of "how dare you?", and stormed out, slamming the door as she went. A moment later I heard the sound of her car as she drove out of the courtyard.

After the adrenalin had subsided, I became furious. How dare she come over for a date, take a shine to me and then get drunk, clearly assuming that I would allow her to stay the night? (In my self-righteous anger I chose not to dwell on the fact that it was precisely the sort of dirty rotten trick I would try with someone I liked.) And then, to top it all, she drove home drunk. I sent a text asking her to reply when she got home.

An hour later, Jane confirmed that she had indeed got home. I had another text later that evening asking why I hadn't been interested in her.

"You turn up looking older than your picture, get pissed, embarrass me in public, and then drive home drunk. What's not to like? You stupid old bag," was the text I never sent.

You can learn more about my equine exploits at www.tidyuponyourwayout.com.

TIDY UP ON YOUR WAY OUT

From Russia With Love

It is a standard practice of mine to ignore an online wink from anyone under twenty-five. My strike rate in that age category wasn't good when I was twenty-five and I didn't think it would improve now I am well into my forties. There is little for me to talk about with people who say, "Who is Gary Numan?" I am not cool. I don't like the X Factor or drink alcopops (although I can knock back shots with the best) and I don't actually know what "reem" means. I am a child of the eighties, and am happy to remain in my generation.

That day, though, I was fuckin' bored, so I decided to take a look. Her name was Anna and she was twenty-two years old (nearly half my age at the time). Not only that, she was Russian and she lived in Moscow. I sent her a quick message saying hello and commenting on how pretty she looked, but that Moscow was a bit far for a date.

Her reply came as something of a surprise. It wasn't the pidgin English response I had expected. She didn't tell me that she had been born into servitude and just needed $1000 in order to leave the country to be with me, where she could be happy with me forever (so please just provide bank account details and PIN). Her message was well-written and considered. She told me that she came from a relatively affluent background. This had allowed her to spend some time travelling around Europe. I was intrigued and we struck up an online friendship.

Anna sent me pictures of herself skiing in Switzerland, walking the canals of Amsterdam, and dining in Paris, all activities way beyond the reach of most Russians. I also found out that she had spent six months in London studying design and planned to come back in a few years' time. As far as men were concerned, she only liked older ones and most Russian guys, she said, were sexist pigs. Both of these were sufficiently compelling reasons for her to contact me.

Russian men being pigs is a fact as far as I am concerned. I have now heard it said so many times it has gone beyond the realms of conjecture. Whenever I have holidayed in the company of Russians, the men do indeed appear to be complete arseholes. Most of them are also built in such a way that prevents me from communicating this to them. There is one point, however, over which my dislike of them turns into sympathy: you don't see many attractive middle-aged Russian women. My jealousy is tempered whenever I see a walrus-like Russian guy walking around with a stunning blonde scorcher because when I look him in the eyes I see his future. The challenges of life under communist rule appear to have changed the ageing cycle, and beyond thirty-five it all seems to go very wrong for the average Soviet lady. This is not a universal phenomenon: when I have been in France, Spain or Italy on business I have met plenty of stunningly sexy forty-plus women. (One particular Parisienne remains the most elegantly sexy woman I have ever met in my life, and she was fifty-one.) In Russia, however, my best guess is that only around ten per cent of women retain a semblance of good looks in middle age; whereas in France, Spain and Italy it must be closer to about 60%. (We, in the UK, seem to sit, along with Germany, somewhere in the middle at around 30%.)

As if by magic, and perhaps telepathically picking up my concern, Anna sent me a picture of her standing next to her mother. It was a pleasant surprise to note that her mum was very attractive too, and I cannot rule out that had she messaged me, she would have got a reply.

It was after I had received this picture that I broke the news to Anna: it was time for Dave to visit Russia. She was delighted and a little surprised at the speed of my decision. We figured out a plan that fitted in with her studies (the idea that she was fitting in a date with me between her coursework still makes me giggle) and I set about dealing with the financial and logistical aspects of a long weekend in Moscow.

I had travelled to the city before, on business, and in those days it hadn't been easy: the entry requirements were formidable and required a lot of form-filling, visa bureaucracy and an AIDS test. Once there, I had been hustled into a van by an armed security guard and driven away at some speed from the airport. At the time, it had not been uncommon for Western business people to be kidnapped and held to ransom, and the fact that I was working for a drinks company made it all the more risky.

Happily, things had now changed and the procedures were much simpler, although the visa was still a bureaucratic nightmare, and expensive to boot. All this fuss for a blind date might look, at best, a bit extreme to the casual outsider. At worst, it might have the whiff of sex tourism until you look at the economics. The cost of the air fare, visas, hotel, taxis and spending money would have easily funded a high-class West End call girl (the price of a lager in a Moscow bar would have funded a Romford prostitute, with enough change for a kebab).

This was clearly a phase of my life where I had lost good old-fashioned financial common sense. But I was intrigued by Anna, and although I wasn't really sure what I was expecting as an outcome from the trip, my gut instinct was telling me I needed to get myself off to the USSR. As a result, flights and hotel were booked so quickly that the voice of reason didn't get a look in.

There is a grey ness about Russia which I found quite oppressive. The people, buildings, cars and hotel rooms seem heavily used and out of date. By the time I laid on my hotel bed in the dull grey room I was knackered. Whilst the process for getting into the country and out of the airport was much simpler than on my previous visit, getting past hotel registration certainly wasn't. Perhaps, in order to empty the airport more quickly, the Government had simply moved responsibility to them.

Anna and I had arranged that I should meet her later that evening at a Moscow metro station, and that we would go and get something to eat. It was not until I left the hotel and began the fifteen minute walk to the metro that it dawned on me just what a risky predicament I had allowed myself to get into. I was in a strange and far from stable country, walking through an urban area that if it had been in London would have had me praying for a taxi. I did not speak a word of the language and could not understand a single letter of its complicated alphabet. My destination was a station on a metro system I knew nothing about, to meet a girl I didn't know. As a final cherry on the turd I had kept my intentions quiet for fear of the piss being taken out of me by family and friends. If I was kidnapped, there was no-one back home who actually knew where I was and why I was here.

On the plus side, I had a guidebook, which enabled me to navigate to the metro, buy a ticket and study the Cyrillic tube signs in much the same way you would look at a spot-the-difference puzzle. Anna kept in contact by text throughout and told me she was running twenty minutes late. Even Russian women, it seemed, were incapable of keeping to a pre-agreed time commitment.

I amused myself by admiring the amazing architecture in the Russian metro system. It was built by Stalin as a showcase of Russian capability. It did an equally good job of distracting you from noticing just how bloody miserable most people looked. I was brought up on a diet of images portraying Russia as a miserable poverty-stricken place and as I looked around me now, I wasn't surprised to see gloomy and depressed people. I amused myself by trying to see how many smiles I could get returned and had just broken into one with a hot-looking girl bounding down the platform when I realised that it was Anna. She beamed right back at me.

It was a relief to find that Anna was real and, more importantly, really attractive. I hadn't relished the idea of being a lone tourist in Moscow, but still less the thought of trudging the streets with an ugly bird. We spent the evening in a bar with a few of her friends, at least two of whom were also drop-dead gorgeous. I could only imagine what they were talking about when they looked at me, as they spoke no English. Most likely, "What the fuck is that old dude doing with Anna?"

Eventually, we found ourselves in another noisy bar that was stacked to the walls with hot girls. It was so packed that some of the girls were dancing on the bar (which made for an interesting view when ordering drinks). There were a few English ex-pat arseholes being rowdy, and I carefully kept my distance, not wanting to be tarred with the same brush. The noise of the club and our language differences made it difficult to talk to Anna, but she looked happy to have me there. We left at about 1am and I headed back to my hotel after we had made plans to meet the next day.

The next day, after a prolonged greeting kiss, we set about on a marathon tour of Moscow leaving no key part of the city unexplored. We walked, held hands, laughed and had fun. In the way she thought and spoke, Anna was mature for her age, and I wondered whether it was because she had been brought up in a different world to me, or if it was due to her having spent a fair bit of time abroad. As the day went on, though, our conversation became more stifled, as it grew obvious that we had almost no common cultural references to share with each other. We couldn't discuss music, film, art, TV, books or magazines so we were restricted to serious subjects such as politics and world affairs. I suppose that at least it gave us something to talk about, but we had a different perspective on everything. We had a leisurely lunch in a café that reminded me more of Paris than Moscow, and as I sat there watching her in the sunshine I knew that, although I was attracted to her, it was pointless to imagine that it would be anything other than a fleeting romance.

Over lunch, Anna entertained me with a humorous (or as humorous as a Russian can be) account of life in Russia since the collapse of the communist state. More importantly, she answered my longstanding question on how Russian men cope with the female population's ageing problem. She told me that there had been a number of suspected cases amongst the country's affluent classes where women had mysteriously disappeared, only to be replaced with younger models. This seemed like an extreme solution to the problem but a solution nonetheless.

Anna spent the night with me. We had very little sleep, partly due to my determination to make the most of spending the night with a twenty-two year old, but also because Russia had beat Holland in the quarter final of the European Cup earlier that evening and the celebratory shouting, singing and horn honking reverberated through the city until daylight.

Anna was good fun in bed but I have to say, on the record, that I prefer age and guile over youth and suppleness in the bedroom department. She had a distinct preference for sex on all fours, (her not me). I didn't establish whether this was a style particularly favoured by Russian women or whether it was further evidence of a long held suspicion of mine: that women like this style of sex because it enables them to fantasize that they are being rogered by Daniel Craig, without the endless visual clues that it is actually me. I have long objected to the term "doggy" style because the word "dog" when used in context with a girlfriend has never struck me as flattering. In a similar vein, I am not keen on the term 'missionary' style as a means of describing the standard sexual position. Given the history of child sexual abuse in the church I prefer not to refer to any of my sexual acts by religious terms.

The next day, Anna announced that we were going to have lunch with her mother. A wave of panic went straight through me. What was the custom here? By having our wicked way with each other was I now bound into matrimony? Was I supposed to take her mother a gift? Did I need a ring? How much would it cost me to rearrange my flight and get the fuck out of here? One thing I did know was there was nothing in the guidebook to help in this particular situation.

We visited a typical Moscow market to fill the time before my date with destiny. It was an interesting place, but even the Old Russian military antiques did nothing to still my mind. I was confident that I had not mentioned or implied any particular connection beyond "friend with benefit" status, but perhaps it had been lost in translation. I could not raise the issue with Anna without running a risk of a greater misunderstanding, so I contemplated my fate in silence, smiling and nodding whenever she pointed out things of interest. In my head, I explored every possible outcome and created a plan for how I would react to each one. If ever there was a time to be prepared this was it.

The jangling of my nerves was in no way allayed when we arrived at the apartment. Anna's mother greeted me warmly, but with limited English vocabulary to express her feelings towards me I could only read her body language, which seemed to say: "Oh, so you're the guy who is older than me who has just spent the night with my daughter who is half your age." I did my best to smile and look enthusiastic but my discomfort only increased when two of Anna's friends turned up and the whole group chatted together animatedly in Russian whilst casting me quizzical glances.

Anna, sensing my discomfort, did her best to translate relevant snippets of the conversation and to reassure me that I was very much approved of. Her mother did indeed seem to be warming to me and, for a brief moment, I allowed my mind to explore a mother and daughter fantasy to kill time while dinner was being prepared.

As I sat opposite Anna at lunch, watching her talking and laughing and wearing one of my shirts, I felt a little sad. I knew, once I'd boarded the flight for home, that it would spell the end of our relationship. Later, however, as I reflected on my Moscow weekend, I decided that rather than be sad, I should celebrate my courage in taking a chance. I promised myself that when I returned home I would carry the new risk-taking style with me into whatever the future held.

Anna and I kept in touch by Facebook and contact became increasingly rare until she wrote to me a few years later to tell me she was moving to England to do a design course. So it was that I found myself collecting her at Waterloo Station on a bright and sunny Saturday morning. I had decided to return the tourist guide favour so drove her to Bath where she spent the day admiring and photographing the beautiful Georgian buildings. I spent the day admiring her. We walked hand in hand, stopping to kiss often, and it felt like we had only been apart a few weeks.

Before I dropped Anna at her flat in North London, we made a diversion to IKEA, the one true Mecca for Eastern Europeans. If ever there was a mark of my affection, going out of my way to walk round that hellhole was it.

TIDY UP ON YOUR WAY OUT

The Convenient Cat

When I met Vanessa, I was on a high. Earlier that day I had returned from eleven days' training in Las Vegas for a coaching business I had decided to buy. The future was bright, and not even jet lag could dampen my spirits. When days like this happen, I am a magnet for everything I want. Life feels effortless; nothing is impossible.

When I'm in this mood, two things principally happen: if I meet an attractive woman I go straight in for the kill, no fucking around; and I usually manage to piss off people who are in the opposite space. That was not my problem today.

I had caught an earlier flight so that I could get home for a friend's fortieth birthday party and as my flight touched down at Gatwick I knew I would just be able to make it in time and that I was going to get colossally drunk. With a long hot shower and a shave, a gentle teasing of my hair with gel and a splash of Hugo Boss, I would be hot to trot. This Essex boy was 'on it' tonight.

When I arrived, the party was in full swing. I clocked Vanessa immediately, noting her tall elegance and what can only be described as pendulous breasts. There always has to be a downside, though, and when my friend Paul introduced me to her, it was clear what that was. When she opened her mouth she revealed an Essex accent that could cut through steel. But as I was feeling particularly benevolent to mankind I figured that I could live with the voice, given her visual appeal, and we struck up a conversation. In no time at all, I knew that I wanted to take things further, a feeling that didn't change even when I found out that she was Paul's boss, which, as far as I was concerned, gave the whole thing a delicious twist. As I saw it, there had to be some leverage to be gained from a union between us. Maybe there'd be something in it for Paul. Could this evening really get any better?

Before long, we were engaged in some fairly drunken dancing and snogging. From time to time, when I came up for air, I caught a glimpse of Paul looking on in horror. On one occasion I managed to steal him a wink. It is fair to say he was lost for words.

Vanessa and I met up in London a week later. She looked just as amazing in the sober light of day, although she had clearly not attended any elocution classes since we last met. I didn't care: there was something refreshing about her voice. Perhaps it was authenticity. She knew who she was and that was what you got. I had spent years climbing the corporate ladder, all the while strangling the Estuary accent I was born with out of me. I had been desperate to hide it, and now she was bringing me back home in a funny kind of way.

We found a lively but intimate Tapas bar on the South Bank, pulled up two stools, and the evening vanished in a flash. I felt relaxed and happy nibbling on indiscriminate little bits of food, pausing every now and then to kiss her. It was late October, and at some point the conversation came around to fireworks night. Then it happened. My relaxed state of mind and the fact that fireworks always bring out the small boy in me combined to lead me to drop my guard. I asked Vanessa to our family's annual fireworks party.

The event is both traditional and sacrosanct. When I was a boy, although my family had not been well off, my dad had always made sure we had a proper bonfire party. More recently, fireworks night had taken on a whole new importance, as it was around this time that my father had passed away, and now that both parents were gone, it had become one of the very few times my brothers and sisters, nephews and nieces, got together. And now I'd thrown Vanessa, like a deviant rocket, into the mix.

"My family's having a fireworks party this weekend and I'd love you to come along."

I'd told her about the significance of fireworks night for my family and she was visibly touched. "Are you sure you want me there?"

I replied gallantly, although an uneasy feeling was already squirming inside me, and assured her that there was no one I would rather be there.

I woke with a start as the alarm went off the following morning and a thought immediately struck me: "YOU FUCKING DICK. WHAT THE FUCK HAVE YOU DONE!" In an instant, I recalled the previous night and the premature invitation I had made.

After my breathing had calmed down, I carefully put on my rose-tinted glasses and examined the situation. What is the worst that could happen? My family might think it was a bit odd, and I was expecting a few withering looks from my older brother, but I figured after all the shit I had put them through over the years that bringing along my date was a relatively minor misdemeanour. My mental spin doctors could work up a plan to handle this one.

What I hadn't prepared for was how I would react the moment she opened her door on the night of the party. Something immediately struck me as not feeling right. She didn't look or seem as I remembered. Oh my god, I'm not as keen as I thought. It was a sensation I'd had before. It is as if something you've known all along but suppressed with all your might comes bursting to the surface. I couldn't say whether it was because of what she was wearing, something she said, a glance, or an action, but she just wasn't attractive any more. This has happened to me so many times that I have long given up the idea of trying to understand what it is that puts me off of people. But I knew one thing for sure: it was now going to be a damage limitation evening.

The party went smoothly, but I was so distracted by the Vanessa problem that I had to use my innate gift of being able to look interested in her conversation, whilst engaging in a more productive internal dialogue. It had always proved a foolproof system in the past, and even if someone were to ask me a follow-up question, I always had a standard answer at the ready: "Well, I think it depends. What do you think my opinion might be?" This answer is odd enough to knock people off-balance so that they would deliver just enough information to give me what I needed. My ex-wife had got wind of this trick sometime early in our marriage, so it had been of limited use with her. Tonight, however, it was working beautifully.

I don't think that Vanessa was aware of my altered feelings, even when I'd neatly placed myself in charge of the fireworks so that I could spend most of the evening at the opposite end of the garden to her, and when we reached her house she invited me in for a coffee. The right thing at this point would have been to politely decline but three things stopped me. Firstly, I genuinely did want a coffee. It was a long drive home and £3.95 for a machine-made coffee at Clacket Lane Services always feels extortionate. Secondly, I have always found a strong female Essex accent intimidating and I was a little afraid of the response a refusal might bring. I have seen friends succumb to the influence of strong-willed Essex birds in nightclubs, in a bizarre reversal of the ritual of cavemen clubbing women over the head, and this made me cautious. Thirdly, as I turned to face Vanessa I caught a glimpse of her ample cleavage. That settled it.

Now, I am aware that the term "come in for a coffee" is a widely recognized code for a range of sexual activity, from a sofa-based tongue wrestle to a charge up the stairs for a night of energetic sex. As I snogged her and enjoyed what was indeed a very good (and exceptional value for money) cup of coffee, I was only too aware that she would be fully cognisant of said code, and I wondered what form her reaction might take if I left to go home.

I did what any man would do in this situation and consulted my decision-making organ. After several minutes of heavy kissing and fondling, the power of attorney had long been transferred from my brain to my dick. I knew there would be consequences as soon as the sex was over but figured that I could deal with them then.

And very nice it was too. But now that it was over, I had some thinking to do. The moment she drifted off to sleep, I began to engage in the challenging process of thinking up a reason not to stay until morning. To me, having sex and spending the night with someone are not in the same ballpark, or even part of the same sport. The bank of excuses I did have, which normally enabled me to leave whilst ensuring the other party saved face, all required careful introduction and pre-positioning earlier in the evening. For example, a simple "I have to get back tonight because I have an early start in the morning" would have catered for this situation beautifully. It would also have left open a window of possibility if things had begun to look promising, as it could always transform into "oh well, perhaps I can just get up a little earlier".

In my panic at realizing I no longer fancied Vanessa, I had completely forgotten to plant such suggestions and now here I was lying in bed with time running out. And I knew that the later I left it, the fewer excuses would be available to me. After an hour I had to admit defeat. The best I had come up was a risky and marginal excuse at best, but if I didn't act now we would have to do breakfast, and I did not want this woman to know my intimate morning habits.

I leant over and gently woke her. "Vanessa, I have to leave."

She was still half asleep and it took her a while to register. "What? ... Why?"

"I have to get back to feed my cat."

As soon as the words came out of my mouth I knew it was an awful choice, and the speed at which she moved from blissful postcoital slumber to alert, mightily pissed-off Essex bird was scary.

"What do you mean feed the cat? It's two in the morning!"

Her connection of real life data and logic had me reeling. "Well, I didn't think I was going to be out all night so I didn't feed the cat before I came out and she'll be starving."

Vanessa was clearly not a cat lover and the hole I was digging just got deeper and deeper.

Finally, she said, "Well, if you really have to go ..."

I didn't catch the second half of the sentence., I'd found the window I needed, and I acted with a speed and precision that, in the darkness, would have impressed a bat. As I left the bedroom I called out, "Goodnight, call you in the week. Sorry about this!"

Once in my car and clear of Brentwood I relaxed. I was safe, and unless she called in an airstrike it was now a clear sprint home. That's when anger at my own cowardice and stupidity crept in. How did I allow things to spiral out of control like that? Why didn't I just say I was uncomfortable about spending the night, drink my coffee, and get the fuck out of there?

In a final twist of irony, thirst overtook me and I ended up parting with £3.95 at Clacket Lane for a frothy latte.

Later that week I spoke to Paul to find out how the land was lying.

"You're public enemy number one. She said something about you being a complete bastard and something about feeding a cat."

I decided to leave it there.

TIDY UP ON YOUR WAY OUT

Shitting on Your Own Doorstep

I was tired. The sheer emotional weight of dating was beginning to take its toll and was taking up more of my energy than was healthy. The single women in my target market were either barking mad, lived ridiculously far away, or were not in the slightest bit interested in me. In spite of my being a nice guy, not too bad looking, good income, funny and engaging, I had been unable to find someone with whom I could have an enduring love affair. All the good women were taken and I was being left on the shelf with all the other damaged middle-aged singles. I just didn't get it.

I discussed the issue with my friend Elaine. Our friendship had spanned over twenty years and in that time she had developed an ability to read me like a book. Unfounded rumours had circulated for years that we'd had an affair, as there aren't many people who believe it is possible for me to have a platonic relationship with a good-looking woman, but it wasn't the case. From time to time it was fun to stoke the ashes of these rumours, just to keep everyone on their toes. But the truth was that ours was just too good a friendship to allow sex to get in the way. Then I met her sister.

Elaine was and still is happily married, but the persistent rumours of an affair between us meant that I was never the most popular person with her family. In fact I was about as welcome as a fart in an astronaut's suit. Whenever I had cause to attend parties where members of her family were present, I would usually be the recipient of withering glances and menacing glares. And, of all her family, none was more capable of looking at me like I was a piece of shit than her sister, Paula. I don't think we had ever exchanged a word in conversation but the absence of any warmth or friendliness in her gaze was enough for me to keep her firmly below my radar.

It was at Elaine's husband's fiftieth party that the ice between us partially thawed. We had a conversation for the first time and found out that it was not necessary for either of us to hate the other any longer. I could sense the idea dawning on Paula that we were just nice people caught up in a piece of mythology about my past.

There was something really cool about her. She had a seaside postcard sense of humour and the Sid James laugh to accompany it. I was pleased that we had, at last, broken our aggression pact and we quickly became friends on Facebook.

Where things should have remained.

Paula was married with three kids and, from what I could see, was happy with her life. My experience of dating married women was, at that point, exactly zero "to my knowledge". The caveat is added because I have a long held a suspicion that a few of the women I dated were actually married but keeping that particular piece of information from me. There was one girl who turned out to be engaged, but in my defence I did not know this at the time. Suspected it, perhaps, but didn't request confirmation until my trousers were back on, at which point I was momentarily overcome with remorse.

A few months passed before I saw Paula again. She was at the Cauliflower pub with Elaine, her husband, and some friends. To say she looked different is an understatement. It was one of those transformations where a frumpy, dowdily dressed mother transforms into a sexy smouldering hottie. It only ever meant one of two things: either a woman has left her husband, or is in the process of creating a plan to do so.

The signs that someone is having, or is contemplating, an affair are usually obvious to everyone but the woman's husband, presumably because the changes happen gradually. The symptoms can include all, or some, of the following:

- significant weight loss

- new hairstyle and make-up

- increased use of perfume

- considerable raising of heel height

- corresponding lifting of skirt hem

It does make me curious, given these obvious signs, how I missed them in my own case. Looking back, my own transformation from husband to bachelor included three of the above.

This time, Paula and I talked for longer and there was a distinctively amorous note to the conversation. With her "Carry On" style of humour and just the right degree of sauciness, combined with an intense stare and confident demeanour, she was incredibly attractive. She was skilful at taking our conversation to the very edge of flirtation.

After this second meeting our Facebook friendship grew and we started to send each other regular messages. Without body language or facial expressions in the equation, things can escalate quickly on social media sites. In no time you find yourself asking bolder questions, whilst having the "only joking" defence ready to hand. It is also a comfortable environment for people to express their feelings and talk about what is going on in their lives.

It wasn't long before I knew a lot of what was going on in Paula's head, and in her life, and soon we had effortlessly crossed from conversation to flirting, and from there to full-on sexting. Understanding boundaries has always been a challenge to me, as my third year Technical Drawing report testifies. If you give me an opportunity to chat with a woman I like, I can easily take the conversation from brands of washing powder to graphic sexual acts within an hour or so. I can't help it. I seem to find myself needing to push social boundaries, always testing how far I can take people.

I found out that Paula wasn't happy in her marriage. Unhappy people stay together for three main reasons: financial considerations, fear of loneliness, or apathy. You may have noticed that I have not mentioned staying together "for the children". It is not an accidental omission. It is not there because it is the shittiest excuse for staying together that has ever existed. If parents don't like each other do you actually think kids won't notice or be affected by that? This is, in fact, apathy disguised as an important reason. I got the impression that for her it was a combination of financial stuff and fear of loneliness. During one online chat I casually suggested that whatever she decided to do she was a really good looking girl and fun to be with, and it wouldn't be hard for her to find someone else.

At these words, the whole nature of our relationship changed. It felt as if, unwittingly, I had moved from advising as a friend to pursuing as a potential boyfriend. And although I liked Paula, and enjoyed the attention she was giving me, in truth I didn't mean to go down this road.

Our exchanges became racier and more regular. I knew it was wrong but I couldn't stop myself. It was naïve, but my lack of understanding of the impact my words would have on Paula as well as my own desperation to find someone, led me to persuade myself that our online flirting was innocent and the comments disposable. I failed to see the coming storm.

We started to talk about meeting up and whether there was any likelihood of us being together. It was an idea that intrigued and terrified me in equal measure. I stalled, unable to bring myself to fix a meeting because of her marital situation. I really did want her but the idea of breaking up a marriage was horrific to me, especially one so close to my inner circle. So I warned Paula what type of person she was dealing with, and that with my track record she would be ill advised to do anything rash. But it all came too late.

The next time we met was at a friend's fortieth birthday party. Paula was with her children, but without her husband. You could cut the sexual tension between us with a knife. I couldn't take my eyes off her, and she seemed to be compensating by acting quite standoffish with me. I distracted myself by talking to as many different people as I could but couldn't concentrate. I could see other men sharking around her, those with slightly less magnetic moral compasses than me, but it was only when I could see that Paula was in the process of leaving to take the kids home that I made a move to speak to her. When I asked her why she was leaving early she shot me an angry-looking glance and said something about not being able to deal with stuff right now.

The next day a text came through from Paula saying that she had left her husband. Panicked by it, my mind raced through the events of the preceding weeks, trying to establish the extent of my role in this monumental news. Ten minutes later I received a message from Elaine asking if I'd heard from Paula.

"Yes, I have."

"It's to do with you, isn't it?"

Her question was more of a statement and although I felt on the back foot, I managed to recover enough composure to explain to Elaine that I was innocent, going on to tell her that I had been adamant that Paula shouldn't take any such action, especially if a relationship with me was the basis of her doing so. Even as I spoke the words I could see the wafer-thin logic. Of course I had been a big part in this.

We spoke that evening. Paula suggested that we meet up but I suggested a more sensible course of action, telling her that she needed to spend time dealing with the decision she had made without my muddying the waters. She told me she was going to leave her husband in any case, but I maintained a steady course. I wasn't being noble. The truth is I was terrified and was trying to buy time to get my own head around what was going on.

Over the next few days I weighed the situation. It was similar to the Rachel set-up, the only differences being the freshness of Paula's separation and the immense risk of alienating my close friends if it went tits up. But, I did really like Paula and, on the plus side, thought that I was in a better place this time to cope with the challenges of dating a single mother. At least now I knew what I was in for.

Procrastination bought me a few weeks. When it felt right, I asked Paula to have lunch with me in Essex, taking the unusual step of declining the hospitality of friends in favour of booking a Travelodge in Romford. Although sex was most definitely on the cards, and by rights I should be feeling excited, as the weekend approached I became increasingly anxious. Part of the problem was my suggestion that I should pick her up from her home, which had seemed an innocent enough idea at the time. Now, though, as I neared her street my mind was fizzing. What if her ex-husband was prowling in the bushes spying on her? I couldn't rule out that behaviour because it is exactly what I would have done if the tables had been turned. As if to rub salt in the wounds, the car I was driving boldly displayed my company branding and contact details for the world to see. This covert operation was already compromised.

Paula came out of her house, walked across the street and got into the car. I hardly looked at her as my eyes were busy scanning the nearby houses, bushes and trees for unusual movements. The second she sat down I accelerated away and it was only when we were about a mile from her house that I began to relax.

Once were in the relative safety of the pub, conversation was still not flowing. It felt like we were engaging in an extra-marital affair, and I was on guard for anyone that might know us, or know of us. The naughty schoolboy in me knew exactly what was going on: I was eating an apple from the forbidden tree. Although Paula had left Tom, I still regarded her as married, and this made what we were doing wrong in my eyes.

Paula's Barbara Windsor humour, loaded with double entendre, rescued us, and I finally relaxed into conversation. When she laughed, I felt warmed. By the time we left the pub the responsibility for my actions had once again transferred from my head to my trousers and we went back to the understated luxury of the Travelodge in Romford and spent the afternoon in bed. The voice of conscience had been suppressed by more urgent matters. I had crossed the line.

It didn't feel romantic (as if a Travelodge ever would be!) or like I was embarking on a beautiful adventure. Instead, the whole thing had a pedestrian and guilt-ridden flavour. When Paula left I took a shower and thought about what had happened. Did I really want to embark on a relationship with all the baggage she came with? No amount of shower gel could scrub off the guilt I was feeling.

Paula endured a lot through this period. Her ex decided to make the break-up as difficult as possible, which included refusing to move out of the marital home. This, in turn, made our meeting up a challenge. We spoke on Facebook and on the phone as much as we could, but the stress of it all was getting to me. It didn't make matters any better when I received a charming message from one of her friends, whose devotion to Paula was deeply touching, saying: "If you hurt her, I will fuckin' kill you."

I found myself inventing obstacles in the way of getting together. The next time we did meet was in the Cauliflower, a place always heaving with people I know. It was a night I had arranged to be out on the lash with my two nephews and I suggested to Paula that we played down our relationship in front of people. It seemed only logical that I didn't want to be seen as the reason for her relationship breakdown, but Paula seemed annoyed at my suggestion and said she had no intention of being my "dirty little secret" and anyway she had already told all the members of her family that we were together.

I tried to limit the damage by positioning myself, and my nephews, away from the usual crowd I mixed with. Paula arrived with Elaine (who gave me a look I will never forget) and sat down next to me. Although it was immediately obvious to everyone we were together, I tried, ridiculously, to disguise the fact.

The following day I spent the afternoon fending off a barrage of questions and opinions on Facebook, text, and phone. There was no escaping the inquisition and I hated it.

Now that word was out, I noticed a shift in Paula's attitude towards me. It felt like she was trying to take control of me and rein me in, perhaps feeling the need to show everyone that I was loyal. On one occasion she told me I had to come and collect her from Essex before driving her to my apartment for the weekend. The funny thing is that if she hadn't told me that I was doing it I would probably have offered. I'd travelled greater distances for Rachel, after all. The issue was that I was being ordered to do something by someone I didn't like enough to obey. So I refused, telling Paula to get a train to Woking. She agreed, but I sensed that the incident had been filed away for later use.

Perhaps my reluctance to play ball was part of the reason I didn't give Paula a whole song and dance on her birthday. The big day was coming up and I had no idea what to get her. I didn't want to make a flamboyant gesture as we hadn't known each other long. My plan was to take her away for a weekend when things were more settled, but I didn't communicate this at all well. It looked like I simply couldn't be bothered. Later, she accused me of being selfish and tight.

Meanwhile the feeling I got that Paula was trying to control me continued. I increasingly felt alienated from her, especially after she told me that since I had changed my career direction my friends hadn't liked the person I was turning into. I sensed it was utter bullshit, as most of my close friends are, if anything, a little too honest and forthright when sharing their views with me. If they'd thought I was becoming a dickhead they would be queuing up to let me know.

The little voice in my head telling me that I needed to end this before I ended up really hating her, and vice versa, was getting louder. However, for the moment I did nothing, knowing that the risk of collateral damage was enormous. It would be like letting a bomb off right in the centre of my closest circle of friends. Some mornings I woke up thinking I wanted to make it work, and others that I wanted to lose her, fast.

On the day we were next supposed to meet and go out for dinner, I contacted Paula in the morning and made her aware of the doubts I was having about the relationship. I then drove to my nephew's in Essex as I had planned to stay there for the night. As we sat drinking beer, my nephew listened patiently, most probably bored, while I outlined the pros and cons of meeting up with her.

The whole thing had disaster written all over it and I felt guilty because I had known it from the start. As there seemed little point in deferring the issue any longer (not least because I could still get out on the lash with my nephew that evening) in true manly form I texted her. For once it was me using the "it's me, not you" line which had become such a hallmark amongst women I liked. Paula tried to persuade me to go out with her to talk things through but, still manly, I refused.

Paula's Facebook status was changed rapidly to 'Mums go to Iceland', which was her coded way of telling everyone it was all off, and soon after, I was contacted by Elaine. Her opinion of me was the biggest thing that concerned me in that moment, not purely due to my friendship with her but also because she was a good barometer to show how far the impact of my behaviour had affected my popularity amongst my friends. To her eternal credit, Elaine scorned and empathised in equal measure, seeing both sides of the story. She may have called me a dick at various points, but I felt, on balance, I'd got away lightly.

Over the following weeks I battled with guilt about my role in what had happened. The fact that Elaine and I had both warned Paula about my reputation did little to assuage the feeling that I was responsible for the outcome. I had been a dick and I knew it. What was equally as troubling was that people had begun to refer to my "reputation". Although I had never knowingly entered a relationship with anything other than good intentions, clearly some work needed to be done to win over hearts and minds if I was going to have any friends left. The first action I took was to vow never to date anyone that close to my inner circle again.

With a heavy heart and my computer perched on my lap, I logged onto the dating sites again.

The story didn't quite end there. Go to www.tidyuponyourwayout.com for the final sting in the tale.

The Greek Travesty

There was a guy called Billy who lived in the same courtyard as me. We didn't have much to do with each other, other than saying hello as we emptied waste into the communal bins or grunting good morning as we got into our respective cars ready for the morning commute. Billy drove a BMW X5 so I assumed he was a knob-head - a sweeping generalisation, I know, but I was confident that statistically I was probably going to be right. In his turn, Billy similarly assumed that because I had bought the stunning centrepiece apartment and owned a cat, I was gay.

We finally had a proper conversation at a communal barbeque held in the courtyard. There we found out that we had one thing in common: being single. We chatted while eating carbonised burgers and compared notes on our various dating adventures and mishaps. Billy was of Scottish descent and maintained a strong Glaswegian accent. If that wasn't annoying enough, he was older than me but actually looked quite a bit younger. But we soon started to warm to each other when we discussed our common challenges.

We both, I discovered, were fed up with having to rely on online dating, and very soon we came up with a plan to go into town for the evening to try out our rusty chat-up skills. From where we lived the definition of "town" consists of the following places (from least to most classy): Farnborough, Camberley, Basingstoke, and Fleet. Even if you are not familiar with these towns, you can probably take an educated guess as to what we were dealing with here.

Over a period of a few months, Billy and I went through the lot like a dose of salts but with little success. Our challenge was not one of confidence but the lack of appropriate women. (By "appropriate", I mean women who wouldn't think we were someone's parents waiting to give them a lift home at the end of the evening.) On one occasion, in a crowded Wetherspoons bar in Camberley, a young lad came up and whispered in Billy's ear. It turned out he was trying to score some drugs and had assumed we were dealers.

Sometimes I had a sense that we lost out because two well-turned-out, clean-smelling middle-aged men could easily be mistaken for a gay couple. There were occasions when we got chatting to some nice ladies, but in all of our encounters I don't think either of us collected one noteworthy phone number. We did work well as a team, however. Billy was always the opener, happy to act like a well-targeted missile. Occasionally he missed target but his primary role was to smash the door open in order for me to charge in and commence relationship building.

Women tend to go out in groups for the added sense of security, presumably because they are likely to meet people like Billy and me. Even today I still find that initial contact intimidating, having to approach a cackling group of semi-inebriated women and feeling like a naughty schoolboy on his way to see the Head. Billy didn't seem to have the same "approach" anxiety, but most of mine evaporated once the door was open. I was pretty good at maintaining conversation long enough to establish whether any of the girls were interesting and interested. If any of them were, our next objective was to separate those girls from the pack long enough to get a phone number.

We worked like well-trained sheep dogs, attempting to isolate any girl showing any signs of taking a shine to either of us. The rules are enshrined in the code of the wingman - a role in which Billy was to fail spectacularly later in this book. As the US Air Force describes the role, "wingman" refers to the pattern in which fighter jets fly. There is always one lead aircraft and another that flies off the right wing of, and behind, the lead. This second pilot is called the wingman because he or she primarily protects the lead by watching his back.

Wingman was a role neither of us enjoyed. Having to keep the extra girls entertained while the other tries to score with a hottie, all the while providing support and encouragement as necessary, is a thankless role. And, as a further complication, we normally liked the same girl anyway. As a result we never managed to see a single opportunity through to a successful outcome.

It was during one particularly unsuccessful mission into Fleet that we first mooted the idea of going away on holiday together. Given our colossal failure rate, we figured that adding sun and sea to the equation couldn't hurt. Billy immediately got on the job, and found a company that offered holidays in Greece, with sailing and tennis included in the price. It was fate. I loved sailing and Billy loved tennis, and we noticed that one of the resorts was reserved for adults only in September.

My experience of lads' holidays had been, up till then, very restricted. When I was seventeen I'd had a week in Camber Sands with a group of friends, which had been memorable because I'd been the only one who'd pulled, and I'd managed to do it twice in the week. Apart from that, my only other holidays with guys had been snowboarding trips, and they'd been peculiarly devoid of females. So to say I was excited, as the two of us drank a beer at Gatwick Airport, was an understatement.

The bus that took us to the resort was not promising. A cursory inspection of our fellow passengers revealed a sizeable proportion that could be classified as geriatric. The balance was made up of other men and a lot of couples. We tried to the look on the bright side. It was early days: the coach was stopping at several resorts, and other loaded planes were still arriving. But things still didn't look any better as we checked in, so we decided to go for a quick sail before dinner.

A couple of hours later, showered, shaved, a splash of the aftershave, smart new shirts and we were ready for dinner. As we approached the dining area of the resort we could hear from the noise that it was packed. We entered, and a second later broke into simultaneous smiles. I couldn't resist a giggle when I saw that the room was jammed to the rafters with women, and I mean jammed. Not only that, but they all appeared to be within the right age range.

We were led to a table that seated sixteen and gradually it filled up. Soon we were like two princes holding court. My best guess is that the ratio was around four girls to every guy. Even more encouraging was the proportion of guys that lacked the kind of social graces that my wingman and I brought to the proceedings. Morons, by and large, and we couldn't have been happier about it.

TIDY UP ON YOUR WAY OUT

Over the following days, places at our table were in great demand. I suggested that Billy and I split up at dinner. With so many women to talk to it didn't make sense our having to look at each other. Our first serious contact happened on a trip to the local town organised by the resort reps. Many of the women we'd got to know from our table came out to play, and Billy and I found ourselves in a crowded bar surrounded by inebriated women. It was a target-rich environment, but I managed to maintain focus on one particular girl.

Her name was Lyndsey and she was on holiday alone. Her pretty face was topped off with an eighties-style wavy perm and she reminded me of Farah Fawcett Majors in Charlie's Angels. (This was no bad thing. A girl is bound to get my attention if she looks like any one of those women who supported me through my difficult boy to man transitional years.) The fact that Lyndsey spoke with a slightly irritating squeaky voice was too minor an issue to trouble me. I thought I recognised her, and it was only after I'd returned home that I realised I had seen her picture on a dating site (which, it has to be said, had been another personal victory for professional makeover photography). At the time, I had tried to make contact, but had been ignored.

The level of focus I showed Lyndsey was admirable given the number of women in the bar. My efforts to chat her up were ably assisted by her being pretty drunk, and as we talked she kept reaching over to undo my shirt buttons. I took this as a good signal, although it began to get on my nerves after a while.

At some point, I noticed that Billy was finding the whole situation a bit challenging. His eyes and attention were all over the place, trying to talk to one girl whilst watching another, and listening to a third. If I hadn't have known that he was suffering from a sensory overload brought on by exposure to a high volume of available women, I would have suspected some sort of seizure. I could see he was in danger of leaving with nothing, so I excused myself from Lyndsey, buttoned up my shirt, and walked over. It was to be a great moment in the history of personal coaching.

"Dude, you need to focus on one girl. You're all over the place. Don't blow it," I said. "So, who's it going to be?"

Billy calmed himself and decided upon which woman he would concentrate his efforts. From that point on, he was away, and like a proud father I returned to Lyndsey, safe in the knowledge that Billy had a fair shot at getting laid.

At 2am, I found myself at the door to Lyndsey's room. I had escorted her back but was a little surprised when she invited me in. After all it was late, we were both drunk, and the invitation could only lead to one thing. It did, and we engaged in colossally noisy sex. It always flatters my ego when a woman makes a lot of noise; it's the ultimate feedback that you are doing the job well. In Lyndsey's case however, her screams made it hard for me (and anyone else in a five hundred metre radius) to discern whether the experience was pleasurable or not. The walls of the block were not exactly built to withstand a nuclear attack, and I imagined people in the rooms on either side debating whether to call the police. The more I thought of everyone listening, the harder it became for me to sustain my performance.

Well before the neighbours were up and about I crept out of Lyndsey's room and went back to the peace and quiet of my own. I was pleased to see that Billy was not back.

I didn't want to spend the rest of the holiday with Lyndsey and was embarrassed about what had happened between us. I tried to avoid her but the resort was small. She was far from happy with my conduct, even crying on a few occasions. I found the safest place to hide was at the tennis courts, which were frequented by lots of fit birds, happily, so I didn't lose out too badly. My tennis skills were frequently called upon by women wanting to play mixed doubles. I was happy to oblige. The fact that I was pretty useless at tennis didn't seem to mar my attractiveness, largely due to the limited number of men at the resort.

Billy was getting on well with the girl he had met. His eagerness to spend time with her resulted in his locking me out of our room on one evening. It turned out to be a piece of luck, however, as I ended up having to spend time with her friends and one of them took a shine to me.

Jane was an attractive enough girl with a gorgeous face, but a little larger than the women I normally make a beeline for. For a couple of evenings she stayed in close, then chose her moment to perfection. I was drunk, and as it was nearing the end of the holiday I was in need of a final sex top-up. So I surrendered willingly and for the last few nights we were effectively a couple.

About six months later I dropped Lyndsey a line on the dating site. I had a meeting near to where she lived and asked if she wanted to meet up for a reconciliatory drink. Her reply was that she would love to meet for a beer so she could throw it all over me.

A firm refusal but, on reflection, fair.

TIDY UP ON YOUR WAY OUT

Eyes Wide Shut

Carly was classically beautiful with long blonde hair and blue eyes. She had the sort of face that should never need to find its way onto a dating site. When we spoke on the phone I thought she had a posh voice for a Basingstoke girl and, more importantly, she ticked my two main boxes: her children were grown up (and she was not looking for more) and she lived just twenty minutes away.

I opted to take her to the Phoenix Inn, a local gem of a pub that had become a dating staple. It had a lovely private table by a small wood-burning stove, perfectly romantic without being obviously so. When she stepped out of her car, I was delighted to see that Carly looked even better than her picture. We got on instantly and, paying scant regard to my financial first date policy, we had a meal. It was a lovely evening, and so engrossed were we in our conversation that we were the last to leave. We arranged to meet the very next night.

I took her to The Lime Leaf, in Basingstoke, a sophisticated - certainly for Basingstoke in any case - and intimate restaurant, the owner of which was a client of mine. I liked to make heavy use of it on second dates, so much so that he would nod sagely every time I arrived parading a different woman. The added bonus was that The Lime Leaf was reasonably cheap, provided I could steer my date away from three courses and minimise the side-dish orders.

With Carly, none of this mattered and I opened the batting by ordering champagne (it was on special but I'm pretty sure she didn't notice). The meal went well and afterwards we walked to the minicab office together hand in hand and kissed as we waited for our taxi. When we got to her house, Carly invited me in for coffee. The next day I headed home with a very big smile on my face.

Through the next week we were inseparable. Carly would come over straight from work or I'd go to her place. We had a lot of sex and a lot of fun together, and our lives quickly became integrated. So much so, that I didn't think twice about inviting her to come with me to Gloucestershire at the weekend to join my friends, Laura and Bob, at the Rockhampton Music Festival.

We headed out to the field in which the festival was being held and at first all was well. As the evening progressed, however, I began to notice some odd behaviour. Increasingly, Carly seemed distant and spent a lot of the time standing away from me. I put it down to her feeling nervous around strangers.

Carly was very quiet in the car on the way home and spent most of the journey either asleep or staring out of the passenger window. This worried me slightly but I had made so many mistakes jumping to wrong conclusions early on in a relationship, that I decided to let it go.

Later that afternoon, after Carly had left my place to return to her apartment, I received an ORT from her.

"I don't think this is going to work between us."

I was aghast. It was WPC Karen all over again. What on earth had I said or done that had prompted this?

For the next three days, not wanting to seem desperate (even though I was) I didn't contact her. Then I sent a brief text: "Are you OK?" and her reply: "No not really" prompted me to pick up the phone. I told her how sad I had been and she said that she'd been too. We agreed to meet for dinner at a pub near her house to talk things through. (This pub was to become pivotal in our relationship, acting as our own personal arbitration room.) Over dinner, Carly told me she had panicked for no apparent reason and she apologised.

With the false start out of the way, we quickly fell into a lovely routine, cooking each other dinner, going out to a local pub for a drink, or sitting in and watching a film. Every Wednesday, her family (parents, sister and kids) would meet up, taking advantage of a food voucher in La Tasca and the "Orange Wednesdays" 2 for 1 ticket offer at the local cinema (a fact I would later come to regret as the fear of bumping into them has eliminated that option from my discount dating plan). Pretty soon I was in love.

I had a new girlfriend and it felt good. Well, nearly. Carly's peculiar behaviour clearly hadn't been caused by shyness on our Gloucestershire weekend, as it was still going on. I knew something wasn't quite right. When we went out for dinner together I noticed that if she wasn't in conversation with me, she would be gazing off into the distance or fiddling with her phone. In short, acting like I wasn't there. It was a strange experience and, depending on my own mood, I became upset or pissed off. My confidence that I knew how to be in a relationship was at rock bottom so I thought it must be something I was doing wrong. My confusion was compounded by her mixed messages. One minute she was aloof, the next she was inviting me to spend Christmas with her family. None of it made any sense.

Before then, I had Carly's birthday to prepare for and I was determined to make it special. As well as booking a table for dinner at the Cricketers, I also had them prepare a beautiful sculptured chocolate cake for her. I spent a whole day shopping for gifts, having picked her daughter's brains to make sure I got it just right.

Not since Rachel had I been so excited about the idea of buying presents for someone.

After a magical evening, the following day we drove down to the coast. As we sat by the sea in the Autumn sun I felt really close to Carly and told her how much I loved her. Telling someone that you love them is a seminal moment in a relationship. It is also something that I probably don't treat with the reverence it deserves. I fall in love quickly and never mind sharing the news with the person. I know it has probably cost me a few relationships but, on balance, I wouldn't change it. There are no fixed criteria for falling in love. It can happen in hours or months or years, so why put a restriction on when you choose to make it known?

Although Carly and I were deeply in love, the odd behaviour carried on. Whenever we were not in conversation, or if we were in a group, she distanced herself from me. On one occasion, at dinner with her family, I came within a second of standing up and walking out to see if she even noticed, but then her sister started to talk to me and, once again, I put the idea to the back of my mind. Another time, I took her to a party where she met many of my friends. They didn't seem to notice that she spent most of the evening standing on her own, away from me, and they all really liked her. When, on the following morning, I asked her if she had enjoyed herself, she blew a fuse. The strength of her indignation was baffling.

At one level I was the happiest I had been for years and yet, underneath it all, I was becoming increasingly miserable and introspective. What was I doing that was making Carly act in this way? Was there someone else? Perhaps a previous relationship she had not moved on from? Was I finding problems where there were none? I kept putting it down to my inexperience at being in a committed relationship. It had been a long while since I had broken the three month barrier and we were well on the way to achieving that significant milestone.

It was becoming so difficult to figure out Carly's behaviour that I started to keep a journal to record what was happening. Perhaps if I could find a pattern I might be able to work her out. Soon, without realising it, I began to take out my angst on friends and colleagues. I frequently exploded in temper and gave way to the compulsive desire to talk about and analyse the relationship. In short, I was becoming unbearable. My PA threatened to leave and my business was beginning to struggle as I lost focus. Something had to give.

We made a return visit to Rockhampton for the village wine-tasting event and, as the evening progressed, I was able to observe Carly's behaviour. One to one, she was intense and lost herself in deep conversations with my friends. Afterwards, they would come over and tell me how lovely she was. But as soon as she was left alone, she would retreat into a dazed state, as if there was no-one else there. It would take a couple of times of asking to get her attention and bring her back to planet earth. I loved this girl and, not wanting to lose what we had together, needed to figure out what was happening.

The day after we got back from Rockhampton I got a call from Bob. He is an interesting character, but can be a social landmine, loving to wind people up and push them to the edge of their comfort zone. It is a characteristic that you either love or find very discomfiting. I consider him to be one of the most engaging men I've met, and knew that he would be mortified if he'd thought that he had genuinely upset anyone.

Bob sounded troubled. "I just wanted to check that Carly was okay. I'm worried I said something to upset her."

I asked him what had happened, sensing what his answer would be.

"She seemed very quiet and a bit distant."

I was relieved. It wasn't just me who had noticed. I told Bob it was probably nothing and that I was sure she would have told him where to go at the time, if she'd been upset by something he'd said.

A few days later, I met Carly to do a bit of Christmas shopping. The excursion was memorable because I had the good fortune to enter an Ann Summers store for the first time. Our sex life was becoming increasingly interesting, which made me realise how vanilla I had been about sex before I'd met her. Suddenly I had been blindfolded, handcuffed, bitten, clamped, and had all sorts of creams applied to different parts of my body.

At first I was horrified at Carly's suggestion that I accompany her into the shop. I remembered a sex shop opening, near where I lived, when I was a child. It had blacked-out windows that were subject to regular paint can attacks by housewives desperate to keep their men's sexual urges suppressed. If ever there was a sign that the world had changed, it was the idea of a sex shop in the middle of a shopping centre.

As I entered, my face went bright red, and became even more puce as Carly started holding up products for my approval. When we reached the vibrator section my embarrassment turned to horror. She was looking to buy a replacement for the device that had worn itself out servicing her single years, and my biggest fear was that she would hold them up against me in order to check out sizing.

The whole experience left me in need of a medicinal drink and we found a bar in the shopping centre. It was there, as we relaxed over a glass of Sauvignon, that I decided to broach the matter of my conversation with Bob. Part of me wanted to leave the subject for later, as I was keen to get home and try out some of the new toys Carly had bought, but I figured this was important.

Carly asked me what I meant.

"Well, I know Bob can be a bit of a dick at times. He phoned me because he was worried he had said something out of order. Said you seemed a bit quiet."

What happened next was extraordinary. She went ballistic. This seemingly innocent question launched Carly into a tirade. It started off quiet but soon got louder and louder. Everyone in the bar was looking at us with interest.

"Oh, so now Bob's analysing me too is he? Everyone seems to want to check on everything I'm doing!"

I don't deal well with conflict, particularly when it is loud and in public. I tried to play down the issue to calm her but she was having none of it. Then I felt the anger of three months worry and frustration bubbling up.

"Carly, I'm crazy about you, and have been from the minute we met, but I notice that you do tend to ignore me a bit when we are out. It makes me think I've done something wrong or that you don't want to be with me."

This rational appeal fell on deaf ears and her rage continued until the point that I could take no more. I walked off. There was no reasoning with her and I felt I was better off at home on my own. I needed my cave.

We didn't speak for a few days and then arranged to meet up at the arbitration pub to discuss what had happened. I loved her as much as ever and wanted to put this behind us and move on.

Carly, although she was still angry, was calmer. "I don't want to be in a relationship with someone who's going to analyse me. I just want to be me."

Her statement should have been a warning sign that things were not going to change, but not wanting to argue, I took it on the chin and said I would try to avoid giving her a sense that I was scrutinising her in future.

I was delighted, as Christmas approached, that Carly invited me to her office party. She had always seemed to shield me from her work colleagues and this felt like an olive branch. The evening quickly fell into the normal routine, though, with Carly being all over me for a while and then acting as if I wasn't there. It was particularly challenging that evening, as the only person I knew at the party was her. On my own, wrapped in my thoughts, I had soon persuaded myself that Carly had to be interested in someone else. There was no other rational alternative, was there? While I was wallowing, one of her friends came and sat with me.

"So, you're Dave. You've been really good for Carly. She seems happier and more relaxed than I've ever seen her. You must be doing something right."

"Why? What was she like before?"

Her friend shot me a look that seemed to say that she'd already said too much, and smiled before making her excuses and leaving the table.

Perhaps I had been wrong, and as if to reinforce this view, Carly came and asked me to dance with her. But, just as was I leaning in to whisper "I love you" she all of a sudden dropped me, mid dance, and strolled off to talk to one of her colleagues. The friend who I had just been talking to saw this so I pulled her to one side.

"Do you mind me asking you something? I'm sure you just saw what happened there. I'm now curious about what you said earlier."

We sat down and she told me how Carly often had a habit of dropping in and out of a conversation. She didn't know why and told me that I shouldn't worry about it or take it personally. (An easy thing for someone to say who is not the one involved with a woman who keeps ignoring them.)

With Christmas at her parentsparents' looming, I decided to make another big effort to show Carly how much I cared for her. My efforts were not insignificant: I made a complicated Gordon Ramsay chocolate and ginger cheesecake for dessert, took personal ownership of supplying the cheese-board, and stocked up on champagne. My choice of gifts was again very considered.

Her family were very welcoming, the dinner spectacular, and yet I had a thoroughly shit day. Carly was on top "pretending I wasn't there" form. There was something else I noticed, though. It seemed that everyone else was aware of her behaviour, most noticeably her mother, who spent the whole day telling Carly where to sit and what to do, as you would a five year old.

"Carly, now you sit next to Dave at dinner."

"Carly, you team up with Dave in the couples quiz."

As the day went on, it became increasingly apparent that there was something much deeper going on and that the family, at an unconscious level, was "coping" with the way she was. It was strangely fascinating to watch the woman I loved looking utterly bemused at the idea of even sitting next to me. If it hadn't have been for the copious amounts of alcohol I had consumed (my own coping strategy) I would have gone home at the end of the evening. (One principle I had resolutely stuck to all through my dating experiences was to not stay around someone who didn't want me there).

Predictably, Carly and I didn't have sex that night. I say "predictably" because, despite her obvious enjoyment of sex when we did have it, there was a complex code that indicated her willingness to do so. If she got into bed, got out her eye mask and put earplugs in, she didn't want sex. If she didn't do those things, I was in with a shout. I am a more than willing participant in sex with women I like. I can be drunk, ill, tired and emotional but the sight of a naked woman is all the preparation that I need to get "in the mood". I have not found this simple biological principle to be reciprocal. In fact, it appears that the sight of me naked actually has the opposite effect.

We got through the New Year but by now I had become curiously fascinated by Carly's behaviour. The more I watched, the more I began to realise that it was not being influenced by me. But it wasn't until one evening in early January that the pieces of the jigsaw finally fell into some sort of order.

Carly accompanied me to an awards dinner for the business franchise with which I was involved. It was a fairly dull affair, but something at least to break up January, a month that is normally just one big Christmas hangover. My business coach Sylvia was there and it was the first time I'd met her, as she was usually based in New York. As well as helping people like me build businesses she also coached others who were recovering after serious head injuries.

The moment I introduced Carly I saw something in Sylvia's eyes, and later that evening while I was consoling a particularly drunk and emotional coach at the bar, I noticed them both deep in conversation. I remembered Carly telling me, early on in our relationship, that she had been in an accident, run over as she was stepping into the road on her way into work. Although her leg had been injured she had also sustained a head injury. I remember thinking it odd that an adult would wander in front of a moving car.

The next morning Carly had to leave after breakfast. After we had said goodbye, I went to find Sylvia. The information I gleaned from her was sketchy and nothing much more than I already knew. Carly had declined therapy for what had been a relatively serious frontal lobe injury. Sylvia told me that the frontal lobe was the part of the brain responsible for emotional responses. Suddenly everything made sense. There had never seemed to be anything deliberate in Carly's actions or malicious in her nature, and yet it was undeniable that her behaviour seemed odd. Sylvia's next words were a wake-up call.

"You know, without help, her behaviour probably won't change."

Whether the diagnosis was true or not, it had the effect of galvanising me. I knew Carly well enough to realise that she didn't like the idea of therapy or coaching. I knew she wasn't the sort of person who would seek help, as she would see it as a sign of failure. She was a 'stiff upper lip' sort of person with a 'bury your problems and they will go away' philosophy. I knew that a decision had to be made.

As luck would have it, the following week I was away snowboarding with friends. It was a chance to get out of the situation, clear my mind, and buy myself some time to think. The choice seemed stark and obvious: either I had to accept that Carly's behaviour might never change and adapt my thinking about it, or I had to end the relationship. Perhaps Carly sensed I was in this space, because whilst I was away she barely responded to texts and whenever I called she was unavailable. On the fifth day, I realised that there was one overriding fact in all this: I loved her. In spite of all the challenges, real or in my head, I wanted to be with her.

On the day I got back home Carly split up with me on the phone, saying she'd decided that she wasn't enjoying being with me anymore and that was the end of that. It was yet another kick in the nuts. Emotionally I crashed, and spent weeks picking over the wreckage. Had I been unreasonable? Had I over-analysed? Should I have acted differently? The questions endlessly circling my head heralded a gradual slide into depression.

Months went by, and every scrap of my focus and drive leaked away. There seemed no way to move forward. Carly had been my one opportunity at happiness, as I saw it, and I had fucked it up in Olympic fashion. Deep inside, I knew it was wrong to blame myself but it was to be some time before the clouds shifted and I was able to move on. If there was one positive thing I had taken from the situation, it was that I had finally proved I could hold down a relationship for longer than a month. Five months, in fact, and given the challenges I think that showed tenacity on my part.

By rights, the story of Carly should have ended there. But a couple of years passed, and a few email exchanges, and then we found ourselves meeting up for dinner. She had been made redundant and wanted to bounce some ideas around, and I had not long come out of another failed relationship so it was nice to have some company. It was strange seeing her again. She was still as attractive as ever, and although some of the behaviour that had caused me so much stress was still evident, I could put it aside. No longer putting myself under pressure to impress her, we had a lovely evening catching up on each other's gossip.

She told me she had not seen anyone else since our breakup and I believed her. I wondered if my getting too close to the truth about her troubles had been part of the cause of our split. We saw each other a couple more times and then we spent the night together. I should have been really happy and yet the pain and hurt she had put through before made me hold back. I couldn't allow myself to surrender to a relationship with her again. The passage of time had done its job.

The Box of Frogs

After an extended break, the lack of sex finally drove me back to online dating. I was still buoyed up by the idea that I was capable of a lasting relationship and that spurred me on. Adopting a workmanlike approach I systematically worked through profiles, even registering on a few new sites. It gets a bit tedious trolling through the same old profiles: women who you like but don't want to talk to you, or old bags destined to be on these sites forever (a sentiment that many women were obviously feeling as they skipped past my profile).

Claire was thirty four years old, fairly normal sounding, quite pretty, and worth a message. This may not sound romantic, but you need to remember that this was production line dating, and my job was to work through profiles efficiently, like a factory worker methodically screwing the caps on toothpaste tubes.

The first phone conversation can be a stilted affair. A somewhat embarrassed "Hi, it's Dave from <insert dating site>" followed by a set menu of questions and an agreement to meet. With Claire it was different. She had a really sexy voice which, unusually for a first conversation, she used to talk about some interesting stuff. We spent two hours on the phone putting the world to rights before (by now exhausted) arranging to meet up later in the week.

I was surprisingly nervous on the night of the date (I think our phone call had got me worked up) and when Claire walked into the pub I nearly choked on my beer. I found her instantly attractive and, although there was another eighties wavy perm going on, she had gorgeous eyes and, yet again, a smile that lit the room. About halfway through the evening I caught myself talking a load of bollocks and waffling a lot, always a sure sign I like someone. Luckily Claire seemed to take it in her stride, clearly unafraid to challenge me, something I found really attractive. There was a detectable undertone that there was something going on in her life, but she was obviously not ready to discuss it so I was happy to leave it at that.

Later, after I'd got home, I texted Claire to thank her for a lovely evening. She reciprocated with a sweet goodnight text. All was well with the world again: I was back in the game.

Her ORT came as a surprise the next day and although, deep inside, I seethed with disappointment, I picked myself up, affirming to myself that I was a great guy and life was still good. The mental bank was full of positive pounds, and there was enough good stuff going on in my life to get me through.

Then, surprisingly, I got a Facebook friend request from Claire. When it comes to women and relationships, Facebook can be a nightmare of tricky social etiquette. Being a prolific Facebook user I am more than happy to share my joys and tribulations with the people connected to me. I am also conscious that deleting someone on your friends list sends the same sort of public social message as a well-aimed brick thrown through their living room window. So it is that once connected, you are destined to remain connected to individuals until one of you dies. And, as a result of this, I have found myself with an over-accumulation of women on my friends list with whom I have shared intimate moments, and I know that if they ever got together they could destroy me.

I sent her a message: "Hey Claire. Happy to have you as a friend on Facebook but I am curious to know why. After all, you decided you didn't want to take things any further with me."

She came back with: "Oh you were a really nice guy, just not right for me at the moment, but I'd like to stay in contact."

So I accepted her friend request and a few days later, after an online chat, we decided to go out for another drink. This time I skilfully managed down my expectations, unwilling to be the recipient of another emotional kick in the ball bag.

I found out that Claire was having a difficult time with her sick mother and having lost both of my parents I knew enough never to assume how different people handle this stuff. For her, I sensed it was a private affair and made a mental note to respect that, as I often tend to go wading in.

At the end of the evening I left it up to Claire whether she wanted to get in touch, making it clear that she should be the one to call if she wanted to go out again. I judged there was a 50/50 chance of it happening.

The following Friday at eleven o'clock at night, I had just clambered into bed when the phone rang. It was Claire. She had returned after an evening out and was inviting me round for coffee. Now for all the ladies reading this book I need to pause here and make something quite clear. As I have pointed out before, 9pm is too late for coffee, so I believe I was quite within my rights to assume I was about to get some sex. Furthermore, this does not make me some sort of sexual predator or "only interested in one thing".

I was tucked up in bed. It was late. Was it really worth the upheaval to visit someone (who sounded like they had consumed a few drinks) on the off chance of sex or, quite possibly, a chat?

Would I be setting a dangerous precedent that I was at her beck and call?

I was up, dressed, deodorised and out the door in six minutes flat, arriving at Claire's apartment twenty minutes later.

She had obviously had a drink or two, but I was pleased to see she wasn't as drunk as I'd feared. She had, however, clearly had enough to bring down her defences, and she was crying as she made me coffee. We sat down and she proceeded to have a conversation, largely with herself, about the pros and cons of going out with me. Whilst engaged in this loud unilateral dialogue she flirted with me, running her fingers over the tail of my shirt.

I found it interesting to have someone analyse me to my face. I clearly had some significant failings in Claire's eyes, but the positives would hopefully be numerous enough to outweigh them. I waited patiently for her to finish, and was relieved when she finally talked herself round, put an arm over my shoulder and kissed me. The kiss lasted so long that I was at genuine risk of asphyxiation. The break for air, when it came, was life-saving. We talked and kissed for a while but I didn't push for more, and although she seemed reluctant to let me leave, with true grit I told her she looked tired and that I should go. After arranging to meet the following week and a final kiss at the front door, I drove home. A happy Dave. I had won the battle for her affections without firing a single shot.

When Claire and I went to the cinema the following week she was in fine spirits. It was easy to feel happy around her. She had a wonderfully infectious smile, and we chatted and laughed about our respective weekends like normal people do. It was only when we were in our seats at the cinema (watching what can only be described as a pile of shite) that things took a strange turn.

I put my hand on her leg.

Claire couldn't have looked more horrified if I'd stood up and grabbed her tits. (With hindsight it might have been worth going for it: her reaction could hardly have been worse.) On the drive home she was very quiet and I didn't know what to say. Then, as we pulled up outside her apartment and I ventured to tell her it had been a lovely evening, she turned on me.

"Look, we're supposed to be friends but you went and put your hand on me in the cinema. You made me feel uncomfortable and trapped."

I took a few seconds to gather my thoughts. The subject of Friday night had been masterfully avoided up to this point but now it was time to raise it.

"If putting my arm around you made you uncomfortable, what happened last Friday must have positively violated you."

Claire got out of the car, muttering that she was sorry if I'd got the wrong impression but that she wanted to keep it as friends.

I was now officially confused. Even after I had been over the details like a modern-day romance Columbo, no piece of evidence came to light making everything fit into place. Ultimately, I decided it would never make sense, so left it there.

Later that week, as I drove home after dinner with friends, I got a call from Claire. She sounded drunk, her voice slurring, and she was in floods of tears. It was only a short detour to her house so I drove round. This time she was much drunker than before so I sat her down on the sofa and made some coffee. As soon as I sat down next to her, she began kissing me, only this time it was even more intense. She had my shirt off in double time and proceeded to strip off her top, all the time telling me slurringly how I needed to be more of a man, and that I should stop doing so much thinking and analysing.

With her tits waving inches from my face, I was not in a position to analyse anything and if I had I wouldn't have made any sense of it. Claire kept kissing me and then pulling away. Next she put on my shirt, and as if by way of compensation for my losing sight of her breasts, removed the rest of her clothes. So there she lay in my arms, stark bollock naked (with the exception of my shirt), explaining that I was a lovely guy, and looked really nice and would be perfect if only I didn't talk so much crap.

I could have taken advantage of the situation, right there and then, but something stopped me.

I pulled away and covered her up, taking the opportunity to get a final glimpse of her fanny as I did so.

"Look, I need to be clear about something. I'm not really interested in being someone that just comes round when you're drunk and want sex (to this very day those words haunt me from time to time. Perhaps because they were not really true). That's not what I want at all."

Claire sat up and stared at me. Then she stood and bent over to pick up her coffee cup (resulting in a view that I can still recall in graphic detail to this day). She began telling me how she was struggling to deal with how ill her mother was, and what a difficult time she was having. I felt for her but knew, at the same time, that when my mother was terminally ill, at no point did I go round to any of my female friends' houses and sit there with my dick out.

"Look, I get that and am happy to help, but I don't want to end up as your Friday night 'go-to' guy. If you want a relationship, that would be great. But if that's not what you're after, I'm not interested. I'll just end up getting hurt again."

She apologised and said that she did really like me and wanted to see where things went. Happy with that, we then spent a few more hours kissing, and I was allowed to make the acquaintance of her magnificent boobs once again. Then, at the point that it was all getting a bit too steamy, we decided to call it a night. When I meet someone I really like, I am quite happy not to rush the sex, instead waiting for a time when it will be memorable, even romantic. Right now Claire was far too drunk for it to be remotely memorable and I don't think either of us would have used the word romantic. But as I drove home I thought to myself that things were, at last, looking up.

A second ORT is a personal record that Claire holds exclusively. The next day, I was about to go into a meeting with a client when I noticed a missed call from her. I dropped her a quick text to check she was alright and, when I came out of my meeting, there was an ORT waiting for me.

As I drove home from work I called her, asking what it was all about.

"You're putting me under a lot of pressure."

I asked for more clarification.

"Well you want a relationship and I don't."

I paused a moment. "Look, I did say if you didn't want a relationship then that was fine. So let's just call it a day."

Three weeks later there was another nocturnal call. I was about to be quite sharp with Claire, and tell her to fuck right off, but she was hysterical, mumbling something about being locked out of her apartment. I was quite within my rights to laugh and wish her a comfortable night's sleep on the doorstep but the humanitarian in me came to the fore.

I found her sitting on the pavement in tears.

I checked the door and realised that she wasn't so much locked out as choosing to sit outside. I sat next to her and we talked for a while before I persuaded her that there was little benefit in sitting on the pavement. As we entered the apartment, I was met with a surprise. A woman came storming out of the bedroom.

"Who the hell is this bloke?"

"Oh, this is my friend Dave."

"What are you doing letting in strange men when I'm staying with you for the night?"

At this point I interjected: "Hang on a minute. Number one, I don't regard myself as a strange man, and number two I was invited over. I didn't just turn up."

At this, Claire's friend stormed off to bed. Undeterred, Claire (remembering that she was drunk and I was attractive) started to claw at my shirt and asked me to stay the night.

I finally lost it. "This is it. You're clearly only interested in me when you're pissed out of your head, so please don't contact me anymore."

Even after I'd left she didn't give up, calling to offer me sex if I went back to her apartment.

I told her I wasn't remotely interested, and carried on home.

Bridge over Troubled Waters

I was rapidly reaching the conclusion that dating sites were not good for my general sense of wellbeing. It was time to return to Essex and raid the Cauliflower pub. One of the principle benefits of this particular venue was that by the simple act of ironing your shirt and applying a half-decent aftershave you immediately put yourself into the top ten per cent of most interesting males. Having teeth guaranteed you a place in the top fifty per cent. (Unfortunately, this ratio applied to women as well.) Still, it was a friendly place and I could always rely on a few familiar faces being there.

I noticed Lisa in the crowd straight away. Tall and striking, she stood out from the others. I recognised her face from the thumbnail photo next to a few Facebook comments she'd posted on friends' profiles, and this gave me sufficient excuse to approach her and open a conversation. What limited knowledge I did have of

Lisa would normally have had me running for cover. For one, she was a big fan of Paul's band. I had always thought it ridiculous the way some women behaved around them. You would think that Muse had just rocked up to bang out a few tunes. Any woman who is obsessed with a band that plays covers in a pub deserves to be given a wide berth but in Lisa's case, she was simply too good-looking to ignore.

I also knew that she had recently split with her husband and that it was unlikely that she'd gone through a sufficient period of "decompression" to be ready for someone else. I went on a date with one woman whose husband had died leaving her with two children. He had been a soldier who had survived combat in the first Gulf war only to die after a short fight with cancer some years later. It was such a sad tale and I realised as she was telling it that I was not going to be able to compete with his memory. I asked her how long ago it had happened and she answered two months. What the Fuck!. Without this period, I knew it was possible that Lisa's view of men, and more specifically me, would be coloured by the extent to which her ex was a cock, knob-head, bitch or slapper. Being armed with this type of wisdom in these situations is a gift of mine. Ignoring it is an art.

One of my friends, who had noticed my persistent proximity to Lisa, felt sufficiently concerned to pull me to one side. His counsel was brief and to the point:

"You do know that she's only just split up with her other half, don't you?"

I was embarrassed to have to answer in the affirmative.

"I would keep away from her."

He went on to tell me that her ex had told him a few things, and because of that he felt comfortable warning me off.

Now, as I was fully aware that there are always two sides to stories like this, it was still insufficient evidence for me to back off. In addition to that, the coach in me always feels compelled to see if I can solve other people's problems. If Lisa did have challenges I felt fully capable of dealing with them. (The truth is, coaching and intimate sexual relationships are not good bedfellows, which accounts for my steering a wide berth around anyone working for any of my clients, even though temptation is often there.)

I have cherished a long-standing Cinderella fantasy, where I rescue a woman from a desperate situation and turn her life around. It started years ago, the day I was sitting in a restaurant watching a girl on the street begging for money. I wanted to take her home, give her a bath, a good meal, a change of clothes and then help her get a job and settle into a happy life. In my fantasy, all I ask in return is that she marries me and lets me sleep with her regularly. Lisa kind of fitted that bracket.

She agreed to come on a date, but it was four weeks before we managed to arrange some time together. In the meantime, I got into the curious habit of calling her every day. At the time, it seemed both natural and enjoyable and sometimes our conversations would last for hours. I could tell that her problems with her ex were consuming her, but although she must have had negative feelings towards men in general, I was flattered that she seemed to think I was an exception to the rule.

The calls continued, even while I was away kayaking in North Wales. There, I would finish dinner, grab a bottle of beer and sit on the edge of a lake talking to her, watching the mountains and the sky change colour. In such a place, I couldn't help feeling emotionally connected to Lisa, even to the point of love.

Sometimes when we talked it was difficult not to fall into coaching mode and we had a few conversations that seemed to really help her see how her thinking was affecting her life. I sent her a self-development CD about happiness that appeared to cause a profound change in her. I could hear in her voice that she was more relaxed and positive. You might think this was a strange way to go about developing a relationship, and yet it felt quite natural. Lisa and I had met, after all, and the physical attraction had been there, so in many respects it was a better position to be in than in some of my online dating experiences.

She lived over a hundred miles away so our first meeting was going to impact heavily on my miles and costs per date. But I knew that if all went well we would make a weekend of it, and to that purpose I arranged to stay at my sister's house on the Friday and Saturday nights.

As I approached Lisa's front door I felt anxious. In the cold light of day anyone can look different, and if a long period of time has elapsed since your last meeting, you are likely to have built them up in your mind, leading to another "for fuck sake" moment when reality lets you down. This wasn't to be the case. Lisa was every bit as attractive as I remembered.

She led me into the house. I knew that her having moved back into the marital home had been an important victory for Lisa and she proudly showed me round. We ended up in the kitchen where she made tea. Whilst she was doing so, I noticed a blackboard on the wall. Not itself anything out of the ordinary: people all over the nation have blackboards in the kitchen fulfilling a variety of "to do" and reminder functions. They are not remarkable objects until you come across one that has "HE CAN'T HURT YOU NOW" scrawled in angry letters across it.

Lisa noticed me looking at the board, so I asked her if it was intended for me. She laughed and explained that she had found it hard seeing her husband when he came to pick up their son for weekends. It was like a voodoo-style affirmation that she would be okay. We drank our tea, my eyes continuing to wander to the board.

Our evening together was lovely. We found an intimate Indian restaurant where we talked easily. It made a change to be looking at Lisa instead of imagining her at the other end of the phone. Afterwards, we went on to watch a band, and we stood arm in arm, kissing frequently. We looked like a couple that had been together for years. (Actually, we looked like a couple that had been together for weeks: it is rare to see people looking that happy after years of togetherness.)

I dragged myself away from Lisa's, after a bit of kissing, and told her I'd pick her up the next day for phase two of the weekend. In what could have been a colossal error of judgement, I had decided to invite her to a friend's fortieth birthday barbeque. Introducing a woman into your circle of friends is always a massive deal. My friends' wives are quite protective of me (my ex-wife had to endure a terrifying ordeal when she first met most of the wives on one of their hen nights. She looked genuinely shell-shocked when I picked her up afterwards) so it was likely that Lisa would get a grilling. And there was no knowing how she would act in front of them. We didn't really know each other that well, it just felt like we did.

As it turned out, Lisa seemed to fit in really well. There were a number of people she knew from Paul's gigs, including several of the band members and their partners, and she seemed perfectly at home. At one point in the afternoon she turned to me and said, "I never thought I'd be back in this crowd." She kissed me and squeezed my hand as she said it, so I took it to be a good thing.

On the drive home, she leaned on my shoulder and everything was perfect. She was concerned that it was too late for me to be driving back to Hampshire and suggested I stay at her house. This hadn't been part of my plan, as I was determined to give our relationship the best chance of working, and my experience had always been that sleeping together this early resulted in failure more often than success. I spent the night using every ounce of willpower resisting the urge to have sex with Lisa, which was an almost unimaginable challenge.

The next morning, as she had to go to work, I left for home, after loosely arranging a plan to get together the following weekend. During the long drive I had a strange feeling that things were not okay. Something was about to happen, and it wasn't going to be good.

Sure enough, the next day the ORT arrived, a classic don't think it will work out, me-not-you-blah-blah pile of bullshit. It would be refreshing one day to get some truthful feedback for a change. Something like "Hey Dave, you're a nice guy, but fat/not well-enough endowed/boring/scruffy"- " -information that, whilst painful to receive, could present me with the option of doing something about it. If a critical mass of women had told me I was overweight, perhaps I would have got to the gym more.

I spent a week sulking and licking my wounds. I was the good guy: open, honest, kind, and full of good intentions. She was the one who couldn't get past her own thinking, and it had cost us both an amazing relationship. It helped to tell myself that anyway.

The reason why Lisa chose the course of action she did will only ever be fully known to Lisa. Sources close to Paul's band suggested that, like some deranged groupie, she had used me to engineer her way into the social circle where they all hung out. I would have liked to have hated her for building up my expectations, only to brutally smash them down. Instead, all I could feel was sadness. I was sad for her, and sad for me.

Swapping Teams

I was still sore from my mistreatment at the hands of Lisa but decided to give womankind another chance. A day spent with one of my clients, exploring their business challenges, had put me back in a great frame of mind. After cooking a curry I settled down with my laptop and logged on to chat with my friends on Facebook. Jane was online.

I hardly knew Jane at all. She and her friend Trudi were regulars at the Cauliflower, which is how she came to be a Facebook friend. I had always made a point of speaking to them at gigs because I had a bit of a crush on Trudi. (At twenty-five, she was way below my target age group so we were just friends, although the fact that she didn't actually find me attractive may also have had a bearing on the matter.)

Jane was older than her friend, but in many ways as attractive, and although I didn't know her as well as Trudi, I had an overwhelming urge to send her a message:

"Hi Jane. You know, I have a funny feeling you and I should go out on a date together."

"Oh my god, you are joking aren't you?"

I had been expecting this response. You don't just spring an idea as radical as that on someone without at least providing some advance warning and building some interest first.

"I will take that as a no then. LOL" was the best reply I could muster.

What she wrote next shocked me: "No, I really like you and have for a long time, but I thought you were interested in Trudi. It would be great to go out."

We arranged to go out together in a couple of weeks' time. In the meantime the normal chain of texts and phone conversations proceeded. (You would think I had learned a lesson from Lisa but it would appear not.) Jane was different though. In fact, she was just like me. I warned her that I tended to be a bit "full-on" especially in the early stages.

She replied "I'm exactly the same, so that's fantastic, it doesn't worry me in the slightest," proving this by bombarding me with texts and calls, telling me how much she was looking forward to our date. This was happening at a rate that matched, if not exceeded, my own enthusiasm. At last I had found someone ready and willing to keep up with the fast pace I love to see in a relationship.

I decided, once again, to throw fiscal prudence out of the window. This had to be a special date. We knew each other, were consenting adults and both wanted it to happen. We had long-since decided to spend the weekend together, and my role was purely to create the environment that would allow us to go crashing into love at breakneck speed. I scoured the internet for a truly mind-blowing date. As if by fate, I received an email with the perfect option. It was a twist on the firmly established favourite from my younger years: I was to make my spectacular dating return to London Zoo.

The zoo opened on Friday evenings in the summer, for adults only. The extensive collection of fauna was enhanced by the addition of music, bars and food stalls. To round off the evening, I booked us a stay in one of my favourite boutique hotels, the Sherlock in Baker Street. I had spent nights there with Carly, Rachel and another woman (footnote: I tried to stick to my rule of 'no married women' religiously but I am only human. You can read about the one time I broke my cardinal rule at www.tidyuponyourwayout.com). Now Jane would be added to the roll call of glory.

Although the Sherlock was a touch on the costly side, for Jane I was prepared to throw fiscal propriety out of the window. Not because I was trying to impress her, but because I wanted it to be special. We had enough emotion already in the bank to make it much more than the usual tentative first date.

The Zoo did everything that could be asked of it. The animals showed themselves, the picnic was amazing, and the atmosphere really special. The only minor fly in the ointment was that it rained heavily the whole time we were there, not a light summer rain but the heavy, cold rain that destroys every outdoor occasion in its path. Nothing mattered to Jane and me though. Under the protection of an umbrella we walked around oblivious to the weather. She was so easy to get along with that I didn't feel the need to think too hard about what I said or when I said it.

When we got back to the hotel we sat in the bar and drank brandy. As she relaxed, Jane began to tell me about her past. As I listened my heart sank. It was a story of abusive relationships and mixed sexuality. Jane had been in several long-term relationships with violent partners, male and female, and, as a result, she had not seen anyone for a long time.

My experience of bisexual and lesbian women was about the same as my experience of gay men. I knew they existed but that was it. I had never given any thought to the idea of dating a bisexual woman, as going up against a lesbian female in the sexual arena is not an even contest. I am only too aware that whilst I have the right tools and firepower, I lack the advantage gained by familiarity with the territory. If a woman had invested even a fraction of the hours I had spent as a teenager discovering the intimate operational details of my sexual equipment, then "me vs. lesbian" was going to be a short contest indeed.

You might have thought that I would have been concerned about Jane having been in abusive relationships, and what impact this must have had on her psychologically, but I wasn't. This is not to make light of abuse but, as with bisexual sex, my experience of it was almost zero. (Once I did get punched by a girl, who was cross because I had spent an hour on the phone one evening talking to a woman who was about to become my new boss. I tried to explain, but the full extent of her fury didn't become apparent until I was woken, sometime in the night, by the sensation of blows raining down on my torso (footnote: if you want to get my attention while I am asleep I can suggest a number of better alternatives)).

We spent the night together and had breakfast in a small café around the corner from our hotel. We spent the day hanging out together at my place and the following day I drove her home to Dagenham. In conversation, Jane was very protective of me, never allowing me to put myself down, even in a joking way. I hadn't noticed this aspect of my personality before, but now I saw how often I tended to slag myself off.

I hatched a plan for the following weekend. The weather had taken a freakish turn for the better, so I suggested a trip to the coast.

"I'll come and get you and we can go to Southend."

She was well up for it, and asked if I would mind popping in to see her parents on the way back as we would be close by. I thought it a great idea: she was close to her parents so I saw nothing but an upside in an early meeting with them.

The idea of meeting parents is often portrayed as a big deal, an issue I am able to sidestep conveniently, having lost both of mine. Many people see it as some hugely relevant and symbolic act but I like meeting people, so I certainly don't fret about it. In my twenties, after only three dates with a girl I was invited to her mother's wedding and was even included in the family pictures. (We split up a week later.)

I was up early on Sunday morning and drove to Essex, buying a picnic on the way and stowing it in a coolbag. Jane and I sat on the sand-coated mud and chatted about life, picking at the food, before walking to a bar for a beer. That afternoon, we stopped at her parents' house. Her brother, who'd been having a rough time at the hands of his ex, was there too. It was lovely to see his family giving him such support. It made me realise the guiding influence I was missing in my life now that my parents weren't around.

That evening we had dinner before going to the pictures. It was gone midnight when we went to bed, made love and slept in each others arms. The next morning I had to be up early to get to work. I kissed Jane tenderly before joining the rush hour madness around the M25 back to Hampshire.

The high I was feeling continued for the first part of the week, and Jane rang and texted me regularly, telling me how crazy she was about me. On Thursday, everything changed.

On the Wednesday evening, Jane had visited a couple of her female friends and now, all of a sudden, she became distant, and her texting virtually dried up. After a few days of getting the cold shoulder, I confronted her about it, and she dumped me. Angry, I asked her what the hell I had done to deserve it. Apparently, I was only interested in sex, it was all going too fast, and she was confused and upset.

She was confused and upset!!! For the life of me I could not figure out what part of the date we just had was only about sex.

The only thing I could imagine was that the lesbian sisterhood had closed ranks and sowed the seeds of my destruction. When they had found out that one of their own had returned to play for the home team they had pitched everything they had at Jane, expressing their doubts as to my intentions towards her (all men being evil and all that).

But, whilst it felt good to speculate that there was a lesbian counter insurgency going on, in truth, I remain as confused today about what had happened as I was at the time. This emotional punch was particularly hard for me. The speed at which things had happened was driven by Jane, and yet it seemed I was being punished for it. It felt that whatever I did was wrong.

Three dumpings, within as many months. I'd reached a new low. In each case I could not see what I had done wrong, or how I might have behaved differently, which only made things worse. It was easy to tell myself that all middle-aged women were simply fucked in the head, but I couldn't avoid one inescapable fact: I was the only common thread that linked the three.

On my next visit to the Cauliflower pub not only was Jane there, but Lisa too. When I approached Jane, she gave me a look that would have killed weaker men, so I kept our conversation short and to the point, after which she avoided looking at me at all. In another corner of the pub Lisa was being chatted up by a guy (he looked like a dork but my normal sense of humour had momentarily abandoned me). It was torture. I couldn't leave as I'd been given a lift by one of my friends. My mojo had completely abandoned me and it was all I could do not to burst into tears.

After nearly five years as a single guy, I had reached a really low point in the game. I knew something had to change, but I didn't know what that something was.

Jane went on to meet and move in with a new partner, relocating to another part of the country to be with her. Yes, it was a female, so it appears that I may have been the backstop for the male population that let the sisterhood sneak past me to score a goal.

Lisa seems to have emulated my track record since we parted ways, with a string of Facebook postings about failed relationships, all of which allude to men being lying, cheating bastards, or something to that effect.

TIDY UP ON YOUR WAY OUT

The Moratorium

I had not been sleeping well as the steady diet of heartbreak had taken its toll. I was bored of telling friends my dating stories, and I can only imagine how bored they must have been listening to them. Life was beginning to feel very difficult so I found a useful mentor and paid him to coach me.

He was very patient, and kept pointing me to a simple truth: it was easy to blame those "mad women" for why I was so unhappy, but that wasn't where the shit feelings were coming from. I had already had to acknowledge that the only common denominator in my failed dating experiences was yours truly, but it was now that I came upon a really useful thought. Suddenly I saw that it was my response to what was happening to me that was making the experiences so upsetting. And the good news was that this was the one bit of the journey that I could control. (After all, I knew other men who were having the same type of dating experiences as me whose disasters were no more than water off a duck's back.)

One Saturday afternoon, as I was looking for something, anything, to break the cycle of gloom, I came across an article in a magazine. Most people have a place where their thinking calms down for a moment, where they can reconnect with themselves and, more importantly, with the little voice of wisdom inside. For me, it has always been places with lakes and trees. I have always been fascinated by wildlife and could never be bored in a field (unlike most of the women unfortunate enough to be asked to share the experience with me). Anyway, this magazine article was about adders, and I don't know why, but after reading it I had an overwhelming urge to go looking for snakes.

I wondered if this was the distraction I needed. I had never seen an adder in the wild, in spite of living close to one of the biggest populations in the UK, so I decided to park my unhappiness and do some online research. What I discovered was that this was a good time of year to see them, provided you were prepared to get up early on a sunny morning and you could find a south-facing slope bordering woodland and heathland. Compared to being dumped three times on the trot, I figured this would be a piece of cake.

The next morning I woke up early and drove to heathland a few miles from my house. I set out across it on foot, using my iPhone compass (be honest, most of you don't even know it has one. The extent of my nerdiness in this regard is not a source of pride). It wasn't long before I saw a slope that vaguely resembled what I was looking for. As I walked towards it, there on the ground, basking in the sunshine, was a beautiful male adder. Tears welled up in my eyes. I sat down near him and took a few pictures. In that moment, this was the best thing that had ever happened to me. Not because I had found the snake but because of what the snake represented. Through my tears I saw, quite clearly, that happiness was only ever a new thought away. It isn't linked to anyone or anything, but is there all the time for the taking.

As I walked back to the car, I realised I had been looking at the whole relationship game the wrong way. It had felt as if there had been a limited supply of women and that if I hadn't rushed in to secure my particular bundle of feminine happiness, I would have got left behind, ending up a lonely figure changing my own colostomy bag. I had bought into the idea that I could only be truly happy when I had found this mythical perfect partner. It was wrong, and in that moment I knew what I had to do.

A few days later, I had lunch with my friend Zoe. We had dated for a few weeks the previous year, and although there had been potential for us, it had been brought to a crushing halt when she had thrown my cat off the bed one night.

My cat got into the habit of sleeping on the bed after my break-up with Michelle, and there is little I can do to stop her. The alternative is unthinkable: having to fall asleep to the sound of my oak doors being scratched or waking up to the intoxicating smell of cat piss on the kitchen floor the next morning. (My cat having perfected the art of the dirty protest whenever she is denied access to the bedroom.)

But it wasn't just that. Zoe fell foul of one of my deeply held principles. As I saw it, the cat was in my life first, and had been the most enduring relationship I'd had with any female since my mother. I am certain there were other cracks appearing in mine and Zoe's brief relationship before "cat-gate" but I still associate our break-up with that moment.

In spite of it all, we had maintained a healthy friendship (and I had never seen her act maliciously towards my cat since then.) Over lunch, I explained that I had decided that I needed to take a break from dating, a moratorium of ninety days. Zoe looked surprised, so I told her the story about the adder. Still a little bemused, she nonetheless set about helping me put some meat on the bones of my plan. Soon we had the rules of the moratorium (to this day I still think her pleasure in setting rules was a little unhealthy for someone who was a friend) recorded for posterity on a napkin.

The rules of the moratorium

To be enforced over a ninety day period (or three months, whichever is longer). During this time you are forbidden from:

1. Online dating – including looking at profiles, writing messages or winking, or responding to messages or winks received.

2. Meeting up with and/or sleeping with exes (Zoe cleverly inserted this rule based on her (correct) observation that I tried to keep in touch with lots of exes. She had personal experience of my constant attempts to try and sleep with them too).

During this time you are permitted to:

1. Approach women and engage in discussions with them.

2. Date these women but not sleep with them, until a minimum of three dates have taken place.

I needed rules and these worked for me. Although strict, they still gave me some wriggle room. I wouldn't have to live like a monk, but the idea of the three-date minimum was designed to break the pattern of second date sex that had so often led to a dumping, in a woman's attempt to rid herself of guilt. For commitment and authenticity the napkin was signed. For me there was to be no summer of love.

I went home and immediately removed myself from the dating websites (this I found hard to do, like a junkie throwing away a favourite syringe). When day one arrived, life continued pretty much as normal. There wasn't a fanfare and no-one arrived to fit a lock on my pants. It took a few days to lose the urge to check the dating sites whenever I was using my laptop, but eventually I nailed it.

After a week, I noticed that I was talking to more strangers. Some but not all of these were women. It was like re-learning the art of going in cold. The vacuum created by not being part of the online dating market was driving me to find other ways to engage with the women around me. At first it was gentle exchanges about the weather, or a compliment about something they were wearing. By week three I was building a healthy collection of phone numbers. It seemed that the less I was trying to attract women the more I was doing so.

Before the moratorium, if a girl had offered me her phone number she would have been barely ten minutes out of my sight before I had called. These new numbers, however, were neatly filed away on my phone. For now, the voice in my head, which I had decided to listen to for a change, was telling me to stay calm and carry on.

As the weeks passed, my confidence and wellbeing grew. Soon my business was surging forward with new clients starting to find me. My wider circle of relationships was starting to blossom again as I was spending more time with friends and family. Everything felt different and much more satisfying. My previous rush to find a woman before I was the last fish left in the pond had been misguided. There was no shortage and no hurry; it was a well-stocked, flowing river. (After all, for every woman swept off her feet and out of the singles market, there was sure to be some guy elsewhere royally fucking it up.) There were plenty of women willing to acknowledge my existence and who wanted to talk to me.

Although I had decided to see the ninety days through, there was a significant barrier to my completing it. Billy and I had booked to go on another trip to Greece three weeks before the end of the moratorium. And based on our previous experience, I knew that holding the ninety day line was going to be tough.

As we sat at the airport drinking a beer at some ridiculously early time in the morning I briefed Billy about the rules of the moratorium. He was amused, as well as delighted at having me out of the game. We came up with a workable outline plan that allowed for a holiday romance without breaking the rules. The principle stretched the definition of three dates to its outer limit: provided there was an hour's break between the stages of amorous advance, the next time you saw the girl again it was effectively a new date. This meant that chatting someone up on the beach, leaving them to go for a swim, meeting them for lunch, disappearing for a sailing lesson, and then having dinner, would put them in the three date window. Technically I should have run this past Zoe, but it took us so long to come up with the idea that we ended up almost missing our flight.

Billy and I opted for separate rooms this time. After a shower and a change, we made our way confidently to the meet and greet session. As we approached the bar we heard the hum of conversation and laughter. It was going to be another belter of a week.

It was only when we rounded the corner of the bar and scanned the territory that we realised something was seriously wrong. The assembled crowd was almost exclusively male. If it hadn't been for their poor dress sense, it could easily have been a gay singles week. What few women there were had clustered together in small groups, presumably for protection from the marauding male packs that encircled them.

It was a total cock fest. The guys were either solitary wallflower types or those would-be upper-middle class, pretending-to-be posh types, who talk and laugh exceptionally loudly. There was one insect-like prick scuttling around the groups, our personal nemesis cock-blocker, intent on dragging every available woman into his circle. He had already got on Billy's nerves on the plane, bumping into him every time he'd got out of his seat, and I was fairly convinced it was only a matter of time before my friend, being of Scottish descent, decked him (at the end of the holiday, he was presented with a special award from the reps for being the biggest letch on resort. The pride he showed in receiving this award says more about him than words ever could).

We finished our beer and sulkily moved towards the restaurant. There, to our dismay, we realised that every woman had been commandeered well before we had even reached the salad bar. I estimated the room to be 90% male, which, even on a great day, were not good odds for me. (Even with my new found confidence I knew my wit and looks weren't commanding enough in situations where the ratio of males to females was more than 50:50.)

After dinner, Billy looked at me and we both said simultaneously: "Fancy getting a cab into town?"

The town was winding down for the season, but there were a few places still open. We walked around for a bit before settling on a small but authentic-looking taverna. There was only a handful of customers but it was infinitely preferable to spending the evening in the resort.

We were halfway through our beers when a group of seven Welsh girls walked in, who must have been in their late teens. Their impact on the place was immediate. After a round of kisses and photos with the owner, they set about daubing themselves in fluorescent paint. When I asked one of the girls why they were doing this, she told me they were on their way to a neon and foam night at one of the nightclubs in town. The next thing we knew, Billy and I were covered in the stuff too.

Fran, one of the ringleaders, wrote her name on my arm, tagging me as her bitch, before drawing a pair of boobs on the other. It was, by now, 3am and when she and her friends asked us if we wanted to go on to the club with them, Billy and I resisted. I didn't feel I was dressed appropriately to be covered in foam and fluorescent paint and part of me was anxious about looking like I was someone's dad (Phoebe still refers to me as her Essex father). We promised to meet them in the bar the next evening.

That set the pattern of the week. We had tennis lessons every day at 9:00am, and after that we would hang out on the beach, go sailing, have lunch, sleep on the beach, play volleyball and more tennis, eat dinner and have a few beers, before hitting the town to meet the girls. It was a knackering schedule as we never got back before 3am.

Becky, Naomi, Bryony, Danielle, Fran, Rebekah and Phoebe were like an entirely different race, and I never grew tired of watching them. I shared almost no cultural references with them, other than a couple of alcoholic shots I had heard of, but I enjoyed their energy and sense of fun. They had no hang-ups about life or boys, that I could see, and the most stress I'd witnessed was their negotiating on whether to spend their kitty on shots or pizza.

On the second evening, I bought the girls a round of shots and put them on the table. Expecting hoots of delight and appreciation, I was surprised when Bryony eyed the drink with suspicion.

"Where did these come from?"

I told her I had bought them and she turned to look at the barman who confirmed this with a nod. I had never given any thought to the possibility of drinks being spiked (it seeming unlikely, other than in fantasy, that a woman might want to have her wicked way with me by doctoring mine), but I suppose that a nineteen year old girl might require a heightened awareness of the possibility. As the week went on I became increasingly protective towards the girls, although to be fair they probably saw themselves as looking after us.

One night Billy and I found ourselves without our protectors. We entered a club and, once we had spotted two single women on their own, we moved into our wingman routine. One of the girls seemed pretty good looking, although outside of the dark club she might not have survived closer scrutiny. Her friend could most kindly be described as a bit of a dog. It was bad luck for Billy, as I soon managed to get talking to the prettier of the two, and he was honour bound to follow the wingman's code to see me through. He did have one advantage, though. Both girls had thick Glaswegian accents, which he could comfortably understand, but I found almost unintelligible.

Both girls were as hard as nails, and in a state of inebriation best described as "steaming". The prettier of the two fell half the length of the staircase on her way down to the toilets. Billy and I watched aghast as she slammed herself against the wall in an attempt to reinsert her shoulder, before rejoining us as though nothing had happened.

I seemed to be making good progress, but out of the corner of my eye I could see that Billy's body language was fidgety. I was going to ask him if he was okay but was distracted by the girl, who was talking in that close-up way which invites a kiss but doesn't quite get there. When I next looked over, Billy was whispering something in the other girl's ear. I smiled at him, wondering if I'd have had the courage to hold the wingman position if the tables had been turned. A few minutes later, though, as I broke away from my girl to take a leak, I noticed that Billy had gone. When I asked the girl he'd manfully shielded me from where he had gone, she said he had left. She gave me the sort of look that is frequently followed with a punch in the face. There were now two of them and one of me. I needed to get out.

"I'm just going to see where Billy has gone."

I climbed the stairs to street level. In the distance, I could see a slight figure in a white shirt running up the road. I gave chase. Once Billy was in earshot, he turned around and looked in my direction.

"What the fuck, Billy?"

Billy explained that when you reject a sexual advance from a Glaswegian woman, you do not, under any circumstances, wait to discuss the matter further.

I was torn. Although I sympathised with Billy, there had been a fundamental breach of the wingman code, and my sympathy wasn't quite sufficient for me to let the matter go entirely. For the rest of the holiday I reminded him regularly of his failings. The Welsh girls were not impressed with him for leaving me alone either. The wingman code was one they understood, and on many occasions I had watched them carefully protecting each other from marauding males or holding each other's hair back while one of them barfed. I'd found it refreshing to see that honour was alive in the younger generation.

On the flight home, though, I was smug. Through a combination of erroneous judgements and a disloyal wingman I had maintained my moratorium. With only two weeks left, completing the full ninety days should be a piece of cake.

TIDY UP ON YOUR WAY OUT

Afterglow

I went snowboarding with Billy over Christmas. Past experience of snowboarding trips hadn't been enriched with much female company so I was almost taken aback when I saw Philippa queuing to get into the terminal building at Lyon airport. We struck up a friendship over the week we were together but nothing happened (not for the want of trying, I assure you). We remained in contact after the holiday and I continued to work my charms.

After a wonderful weekend spent birdwatching on the Suffolk marshes (she lived in Ipswich, two hours' drive on a good run), we continued to fall more deeply in love by the day. Philippa turned out to be my one true soulmate. After six months, she moved from Suffolk and we bought a place together: a dreamy cottage surrounded by stunning countryside. We married a year to the day after our eyes first met on that cold airport tarmac. Every day I wake up, look into her eyes and fall in love all over again. We spend our days gardening, decorating our home, hunting for antiques and travelling together. So the story ends just as it is supposed to, how I have been told it should throughout my life. I finally have the blissfully happy existence of my married friends.

If this were all true, I would probably never have felt the need to write this book. The fact is, in my relationship with Philippa there were lovely weekends and there were truly shit ones. Those times we spent together when we both happened to be in positive mental states were beautiful but, in the end, there were too many long drives that ended up with my looking into the eyes of someone's face that said anything but "I love you". In short, the relationship ended up following the same pattern as so many of the previous ones.

One afternoon, as I sat in my local coffee shop, I was pondering why so many people were single. If marriage or long-term relationships were the key to happiness, why were people choosing to abandon them, and why were so many married people so bloody miserable? Being in a relationship was a different feeling to being single. That didn't mean it was better. In my six years as a single bloke, I had met a bunch of different women, had countless experiences, good and bad. What would my life have been like if I'd been in the same relationship for that period? Better, worse, the same? I didn't know the answer, but I realised how lucky I was to have had the experiences.

I have accumulated more experience of dating, women and sex than I had in the whole preceding thirty-nine years, by a factor of many times. Through this experience it would be fair to say I learned a lot about relationships and a hell of a lot about myself.

It may be easy for you be outraged by my actions but every one of them was shaped by trying to find someone special to spend the rest of my life with. As with everyone there are things I have done that do not make me proud, but there is nothing I would go back and change. All of these experiences have given me an opportunity to learn to be a better person. Whether I absorbed all of those lessons remains to be seen.

The six years have left me with a host of female acquaintances, many of whom will be lifelong friends and some who will be lifelong enemies. I have fallen in love more times than I can remember, I've dumped, been dumped, helped people, hurt people, cheated, lied, cried, laughed, frustrated and been frustrated.

Dating in middle age is not the same as dating in your twenties. Unfortunately many of us who are in the game suffer from a dangerous delusion. We think we are still young. One forty-two year old average looking woman who is a friend on my Facebook page asked me if my twenty-four year old nephew was single and available. It made me laugh and beautifully illustrated my point at the same time. She was clearly suffering from a level of delusion that is likely to leave her trapped in singledom for some while. For one, if my nephew did date her he would have one objective: to shag her and then get away as quickly as possible. This, I am led to believe is the last type of treatment most women claim to want. Secondly it shows that she needs a mirror before she needs a subscription to a dating site.

Whilst I think I have aged well I am not under such delusions, especially when you consider I came from a poor start. I was a skinny, spotty odd kid with a big nose and a predilection for what now seem ridiculously large glasses. The ageing process and its filling out and re-shaping of my features have been largely kind. There is perhaps a little more "filling out" than I would like but on the whole I am pleased with the cards dealt to me. That said I won't be actively pursuing twenty-four year olds any time soon.

If you asked most of the women in this book to recall their version of these events I guarantee they will reveal a completely different perspective to the one I have given - that is what we humans have to put up with. We create our experience of relationships in our heads and in our thinking. We might be in the same relationship but chances are we will be seeing things very differently.

People pay good money to ride the type of rollercoaster I'd been on for the past six years. We love the fear, the excitement, and the sheer relief afterwards. What if some of us like living our lives in this way? And if so, why stop?

It seems I am uniquely built for this type of living. I throw myself head-first into everything I do. I try everything and quickly dispense with anything that doesn't work for me. I don't like stability and vigorously resist routine.

And so, after six years, travelling over 50,000 miles and spending around £40,000 on dating and related activities, I've ended up back where I started. But the great thing is I don't regret a moment , even the sadness, because without these experiences I wouldn't have figured out that I don't need a relationship to be happy.

And I've realised that the very things I used to see as my failings are actually my greatest strengths. For me, I spent far too long thinking it was about the destination when all the time it was the journey. What about you?

P.S. To everyone I have ever dated or been involved with: if you loved me, hated me, wanted me or couldn't wait to get away from me, thank you for being part of this astonishing journey. And to the little snake on the heath: I hope you are alive and well.

I really hope you have enjoyed my book. If you have, visit www.tidyuponyourwayout.com where you will find some writing that never made the book and some further insights into some of the stories. You can connect with me on Facebook (just like the 'Tidy up on your way out' page) and Twitter (@TidyUpOnWayOut).

Also – Please tell your friends about the book and post your review on Amazon.

Thank you so much for reading my story!

Dave.

A word about breasts

As an admirer of women's breasts and also someone who has a vested interest in maintaining as wide a female gene pool as I can (given my own limited looks) I wanted to bring Bosom Buddies to your attention. There have been several women I have dated and that I count as friends who have battled Breast Cancer. In fact there have been enough cases I am aware of to compel me to raise awareness of the work of Bosom Buddies. Please take a visit to their website www.Bosombuddiesuk.com where you will find some really useful information about checking for Breast Cancer as well as an additional contribution from me about BREASTS.

ABOUT DAVE

Born to a working class family in Essex, Dave endured a boringly happy childhood. His educational potential was largely squandered by his desire to spend his days pissing about. As a result his clerical career started at sixteen with the civil service and then the NHS.

He sustained a lifestyle that saw him just about earning enough to keep himself in beer and fags until his 'career' hit a seam of good luck and he applied for, and got, a job two grades higher. This was the beginning of a hugely successful (but hopelessly dull) corporate career.

Never confident with women, he failed to ask out pretty much every woman he fancied and ended up with an impressive catalogue of female friends. Finally summoning enough courage to alter this state of affairs, his life became one of happy mediocrity with a well paid job and an attractive but underappreciated fiancé. The relationship was to last five years. They never married (there was some confusion between the parties about what being engaged meant.)

Excitement was provided by a brief flirtation with motorbikes.

Then at 28 he confronted mortality when his mother died. Whilst on the surface he coped well with the grieving process, his life turned 360 degrees. His coping strategy was to take a job with lots of international travel and to engage in every adrenalin sport known to man.

This wild ride lasted three years before he met, fell in love with, and within a year, married his wife.

Dave took to marriage like a snake takes to roller skates. His attempts to surrender to domestic routine, over adventure and unpredictability, were largely unsuccessful and led to an expanding waistline, a penchant for Austin Reed clothes and finally, eight years in, the end of the marriage.

Adapting to single life pretty well, all things considered, he embarked on a journey of indulging, his mid life crisis. Snowboarding, sailing, flash cars and clothes, dating any woman that showed even the remotest spark of interest and partying hard (well, as hard as his social circle and limited looks allowed)

His career was the one area where success continued to seem assured, so inevitably three years after his divorce he went to work dismantling that. He engineered redundancy from a six figure salary + bonus + benefits and headed into the world with no idea what to do next.

After six months of having fun, he trained, and established himself as a self employed Business Coach, a role he has stayed with to date. Through coaching he began to access new ideas and ways of looking at the world and finally finds himself content.

Throughout his life only three things have been constant...the support of his family and closest friends, his love of nature and Gary Numan.

Made in the USA
Charleston, SC
23 August 2013